D1267654

100 Tough Questions for Japan

装幀 ● 菊地信義
装画 ● 野村俊夫

執筆 ● 鶴田佳子
　　　佐近忠宏
　　　井上恵一

翻訳 ● Lucinda Ikuko Otsuka
イラスト ● 青木宜人

編集 ● 翻訳情報センター

Published by Kodansha International Ltd.,
17-14 Otowa 1-chome, Bunkyo-ku, Tokyo 112-8652.
No part of this publication may be reproduced
in any form or by any means without permission
in writing from the publisher.
Copyright © 1996 Kodansha International Ltd.
All rights reserved. Printed in Japan.

First Edition 1996

ISBN4-7700-2091-0
98 99 00   15 14 13 12 11

英語で話す「日本の謎」Q&A

外国人が聞きたがる100のWHY

100 Tough Questions for Japan

板坂 元 [監修]

はじめに

　日本人は,明治維新以来,近代化・西欧化が進んできていることに自信を抱いている。たしかに,西欧についての情報は,他のアジアの諸国に比べて豊富かつ十分に進んでいる。

　が,色々な点で,外国人から質問されると「それは気がつかなかった」と頭を傾げることが少なくない。

　たとえば,日本人は他人の部屋のドアをノックする際,疑うことなく当然のこととして,中指を使って2回ノックする。けれども,欧米では3回から4回ノックするのが常識になっているのに,なぜ2回しかノックしないのかについて日本人は無関心だし,質問されても答えられない。

　また,中国人の場合は3回ノックするのが普通なのに,日本人は疑問を抱くことがない。中国語なら「在不在(いるかい?)」という言葉に対応する非言語通信なのだが,日本人は「なぜ2回なのか」について答えられない。

　似たようなことで,日本人は交通信号のグリーンを「あお」と呼んでいる。その影響のためか,日本の交通信号のグリーンは,都市によってはブルーと呼びたくなるほどブルーに近くなっている。それは「あお」という言葉と「みどり」がハッキリ区別されていないせいなのか。

　そういう例を見ていると,異文化間のギャップは外国人の出した質問に微妙に複雑さを呈している。近代化し西欧化した日本人は,その点を自らに問いかけて疑問を解き明かしていく必要が大いにあるようだ。

板坂　元

PREFACE

The Japanese are convinced that they have come a long way in modernization and westernization since the Meiji Restoration. Compared to other Asian countries, there is a wealth of up-to-date information about the West in Japan.

However, when a Japanese is asked a question posed by a non-Japanese, it is not rare in many instances for a Japanese to cock his or her head and say, "That's something I've never thought about."

For example, when knocking on a door to someone's room, the Japanese, without even stopping to think about something that comes naturally to them, would knock twice using the knuckle of their middle finger while Westerners would knock three or four times. The Japanese show little interest when asked why only twice and are unable to come up with an answer.

The Japanese do not question why the Chinese also knock three times. In Chinese, "Are you there?" is written in three characters, 在不在. Knocking three times is a form of non-language communication corresponding to the three characters. The Japanese however, are unable to give an answer to the question, "Why two times?"

In a similar vein, the Japanese refer to a green traffic light as blue. Perhaps due to this influence, there are cities where the green looks so much like blue that one is tempted to call it blue. This is perhaps due to the fact that in Japanese, there is no clear distinction between blue and green.

These examples depict a subtle complexity in the questions posed by non-Japanese reflecting a cross-cultural gap. There is a great need for the Japanese, who have become modern and western in their outlook, to field questions themselves to clarify these baffling queries.

Itasaka Gen

目 次

目次の頭に＊印のつい
ている項目が、別売の
カセットテープに収録
されているものです。

CONTENTS

2. 日本人のマナーと行動のふしぎ　　59

2. Puzzling Manners and Behavior of the Japanese 59

3. 日本人の好みのふしぎ　95

4. 日本人の性格のふしぎ　117

3. Puzzling Tastes
of the Japanese   **95**

4. The Puzzling Character
of the Japanese   **117**

7. 日本の結婚式・葬式のふしぎ　　　　　　213

1

日本人の
日常の生活と習慣の
ふしぎ

Puzzling Features of
Everyday Life and Customs
in Japan

Question なぜ，日本では年賀状を出さねばならないのですか？

Answer　英米のクリスマス・カードの習慣と同じと言ってもいいかも知れませんが，宗教とは関係がないところが日本独特です。

　それに，郵政省が「お年玉つき年賀葉書」を発行して熱をあおっているわけですから，集団で行動をしていると安心する，という日本人の習性を表した現象かもしれません。

　日本では，年始の挨拶をする習わしが平安時代からあり，当時から正月には，主君，父母，親戚，知人，師匠，近隣の人々，上役などに挨拶に行っています。

　江戸時代には，武士の世界は当然のこと，町人の世界でも，正月に扇子や手拭い，浮世絵（時には春画！）などの刷り物を持って年始に回っています。この習慣は明治の初期まで根強くあり，現代でも家父長的なしきたりが強い地域では欠かせません。

　しかし，明治時代になって，郵便が簡単に送れるようになると，年始の挨拶には年賀状が一番便利と誰もが気付きました。そして，年賀郵便の制度はすでに1899年に作られているのです。「お年玉つき年賀葉書」は太平洋戦争後の1948年の誕生です。

　日本全国で出される年賀状の数は，今では，

Q Why are New Year's cards sent in Japan?

A Sending New Year's cards can be regarded as being similar to the custom of sending Christmas cards in the West, but with no religious significance in Japan.

The Ministry of Posts and Telecommunications incites enthusiasm for sending these cards by printing a lottery number on each card. This may perhaps be a phenomenon reflecting the penchant of the Japanese quick to pick up on group-oriented activities because of the security offered by the group.

The custom of paying courtesy calls at New Year to one's lord, parents, relatives, acquaintances, teachers, people in the neighborhood, one's superiors, etc. began during the Heian period (794–1185).

During the Edo period (1600–1868), not only was it expected of the warriors, but also of the merchants to make their round of calls at New Year bringing items such as folding fans, hand towels and ukiyoe prints (sometimes pornographic!). This custom took firm root and continued until the early Meiji period (1868–1912) and is still practiced today in areas where patriarchy is firmly entrenched.

Sending by mail became expedient during the Meiji period and many people capitalized on this convenient means of sending New Year's cards to fulfill their obligation of making New Year's calls. The New Year's card postal system was set up as early as 1899 and cards with lottery numbers came into being in 1948 after the end of World War II.

The total number of New Year's cards delivered on New

　元旦の1日に配達される数だけでも26億5000万枚(1996年)。

　本来，年賀状は1月2日に書くものですが，今では12月に入ったら宛名を書き始める人も多く，また，文面は印刷しただけという年賀状も多くなりましたし，確かに形骸化したことは認めねばなりません。

　しかし，よく見ていただくと，毎年の干支をデザインに取り入れて版画を作ったり，それぞれ様々な工夫をしており，見ていて実に楽しいものでもあります。

　最近では，自分が好きな画像や写真を取り入れて，自分が好きな年賀状を作ることができるワープロやパソコンのソフトも，数多く出回っています。

　年賀葉書の収入は，国の福祉事業にも使われており，大きな社会的な役割さえも果たすようになっています。

Year's Day in 1996 throughout Japan reached an astonishing 2.65 billion.

New Year's cards were formerly written on January 2, but many people nowadays begin to write the receiver's address in December. Also, many resort to printed messages, evidence that this custom has become but a mere formality.

The designs of the different zodiacs every year are incorporated onto the cards. The designs are truly diverse and original utilizing wood block prints and other artistic devices. These are indeed a pleasure to see.

There are many different word processors and computer software that contain images and photos that can be utilized to create a personalized card.

New Year's cards have also come to fulfill a great role in society; a part of the proceeds is used for welfare work in Japan.

Question なぜ，1年の間にお中元，お歳暮と2度も贈り物をしなければならないのですか？

Answer 　これは日本人が古くから，1年を2つに分けて生活していたことに理由があります。

　「歳暮」は年の暮れという意味で，年が明けて先祖の霊を祀り，縁者が食べ物を持ち寄って集まり食事をしていました。これが，現代のお歳暮および正月の習慣に結びついています。お歳暮の贈答の品物に，現在でもサケやブリなどの生物（なまもの）が選ばれるのは，この習慣の名残です。

　「中元」という言葉は陰暦の7月15日のことで，この日にも縁者が集まり，先祖の霊を祀り，一緒に食事をしています。これが現代のお中元，お盆の習慣の始まりです。

　1年の前半と後半が，祖先の霊を祀ることから始まり，それぞれ春と秋の彼岸など，同じような行事で繰り返されていたのです。というわけで，お歳暮，お中元という1年に2回も大きな出費をしなければならない習慣が残ってしまいました。

　しかし，今はなぜ，上役や，仕事の得意先などにまで物を贈る習慣になってしまったのでしょうか。日本の社会が家父長制，身分などの上下関係に縛られていた時代から，個々人の連合体に移行する中で，血縁の関係よりも，自らが関わる社会的な人間関係を円滑にすることが重要になってきたからです。

Q Why are gifts sent twice a year at midyear and at the year-end?

A The Japanese from long ago, have carried on with everyday life regarding the year to be divided into two parts.

Seibo means the end of the year. The end-of-the-year custom and the New Year's custom of today are based on a ceremonial feast to pray for the repose of one's ancestors with relatives gathering and bringing food. As a vestige of this custom, perishables such as salmon and yellow tail are often chosen today as gifts.

Chūgen (midyear) refers to July 15 according to the lunar calendar. Relatives also gathered on this day to partake of a meal to offer prayers to their ancestors. This evolved into the present day midyear and *obon* (a Buddhist festival of the dead) customs.

The same formalities are repeated during the vernal and autumn equinox during the first half and second half of the year which evolved from these ceremonies to pray for the repose of one's ancestors. A remnant of this custom obligates one today to be burdened financially twice a year with *ochūgen* and *oseibo*.

The reason why this custom is now directed towards gifts to one's superiors and customers one regularly does business with is because it has become important to grease human relationships other than with one's relatives that the Japanese are confronted with socially, stemming from a shift from a society bound by patriarchy and a strict pecking order to one of the present based on individual affiliation.

Question　なぜ，4と9という数が嫌がられるのですか？

Answer

　　英語にも不吉な数字がありますね。the thirteen superstition と言って13を忌み嫌います。これはキリストの最後の晩餐に参加した人数が13人だったからだそうですが，実はギリシアでピタゴラスが生きていた時代から，13は「よくない数字」と言われていたようです。

　　それにしても，キリスト教信者でもない日本人まで，「13日の金曜日」を嫌っているのは面白い現象です。キリスト教徒でもないのにクリスマスを祝うのと同じでしょうか。

　　さて，日本人が4と9の数字を嫌うのは，日本語の音から来るものです。

　　4は［shi］と発音されますから，同じ音の「死」（＝death）を連想させるからです。また，9は［ku］と発音されますから，同じ音の「苦」（＝agony, torture）を連想させるので，9も嫌われます。

　　従って，特に病院では，病気で死と戦っている人も多いわけですから，病室などにこの2つの数字を使うことを嫌います。

　　日本の旅客機の席には，4番もありませんし，13番もありません。また，日本のビルでも，13階を表示せずに，12階を12a，13階を12bとしているところもあります。

Q Why are the numbers 4 and 9 disliked?

A There are also unlucky numbers in the English language. Derived from the thirteen superstitions, the number 13 is abhorred. Although it is said that the dislike for the number 13 originated with the Last Supper Jesus shared with 13 people, the number 13 was considered to be unlucky from the time of Pythagoras in Greece.

It is interesting to note that the Japanese, although not Christians, dislike Friday the 13th while at the same time celebrate Christmas.

The reason for the dislike for the numbers 4 and 9 derives from its pronunciation. Four is pronounced *shi* which is associated with death pronounced the same way. Nine is pronounced *ku* which is associated with agony or torture pronounced the same way.

There are many desperately ill hospitalized patients who dislike having these numbers on their hospital room door.

There are no seats with the numbers 4 and 13 on passenger planes of the All Nippon Airways. There are also buildings in Japan with no thirteenth floor. The twelfth floor is designated as 12a and the thirteenth floor as 12b.

Question なぜ，神社では拝むときに手をたたくのに，お寺では合わせるだけなのですか?

Answer

　手をたたくことを「拍手[はくしゅ]」と言います。[かしわで]とも読み，こう読むと，神殿の前で日本神道の神を拝むときに手をたたくことを意味します。

　古くは，朝廷における儀式の際に，また，偉い人から贈り物をもらう時などにも拍手をしたと言われます。

　拍手のやり方は2回とか，4回とか，拝む対象や宗派によって違っていたようです。出雲大社や宇佐神宮では4回たたきます。伊勢神宮では八開手と言って，8度打つ場合もあります。

　一般に，神社でお参りするときは，ポン，ポン，と2回たたくのが普通です。

　さて，お寺ではどうしてたたかないのかということですが，仏教には「合掌[gasshou]」という言葉があり，これが仏教における礼法の1つとなっているのです。

　合掌は，指と両方の掌を，顔あるいは胸の前で合わせて，仏様や亡くなった人を拝む動作を言います。仏教では右手は仏様，左手は迷いの世界にある，あらゆる生類を表すとされ，両手を合わせることによって，仏と合体した成仏という姿を表しているのです。

Q Why are the hands clapped when praying at shrines (Shintoism) and placed together when praying at temples (Buddhism)?

A The reading of the kanji to clap one's hands is *hakushu*. This kanji can also be read as *kashiwade* meaning to clap one's hands in prayer at a Shinto shrine.

It is said that in ancient times, people clapped their hands at ceremonies held at the Imperial Court or when receiving a gift from a person in a high position.

The number of claps, whether it is two or four, depends on the object of worship and the religious sect. The hands are clapped four times at Izumo Shrine and at Usa Shrine, while there are occasions when the hands are clapped eight times, referred to as *yahirade*, at Ise Shrine.

Generally, the hands are usually clapped twice when visiting a shrine.

The hands are not clapped at temples because of *gasshou* (putting the palms together), a Buddhist term denoting one of the Buddhist decorums.

Gasshou refers to a gesture of placing the fingers and the palms of both hands together in front of one's face or chest to pray for Buddha and people who are deceased. In Buddhism, the right hand represents Buddha and the left hands represents all living things not in a state of spiritual enlightenment. Placing both hands together represents a pose of a spiritual awakening in unity with Buddha.

Question　なぜ，日本では相手にすぐお酒をついであげるのですか？

Answer

　日本語で『杯を交わす』と言うと，酒を共にして約束を固め合うことを意味します。他にも，上の人から目をかけてもらうという意味で『杯を頂戴する』と言うなど，杯を用いた表現がたくさんあります。

　一般にどの社会でも，飲食を共にするということは，共同体の一員としての確認の儀式ですが，日本では酒を介した付き合いが基本になることが多く，いっしょにお酒を飲んでいるときは，相手の杯やコップが空になっていたら，ちゃんと満たしてあげるのが礼儀なのです。

　外国のパーティーなどではホストがお酒をすすめてくれますが，たいていは最初の1回だけで，後は客の自由，というルールに比べると，日本人のお酒のすすめ方は，外国人にとってはしつこいと映るのでしょう。

　それに，日本式の宴会の席で，偉い人の前でかしこまってお酒をついでいる姿も，外国人の目に不思議に映ることでしょう。

　しかし，和室の宴会の席では，左右から四角い部屋の中に四角い囲みを作るように，上位の客の順に座るのが習わしです。偉い人にご挨拶をするということになると，自分の席を立って，部屋の中央から相手の席の前に進まざるをえないのです。

Q. Why are the Japanese always so quick to pour sake into another's sake cup?

A There are many terms referring to sake in Japanese. The expression, *sakazuki wo kawasu* means to solidify a promise to each other by drinking sake together. Another expression concerning sake is, *sake wo chōdai suru* or to be looked after by one's superior.

In any society, eating and drinking together is a formality of corroborating that one is a member of that communal society, but in Japan, drinking sake together is based on an intent to become acquainted with the other. When drinking sake together, it is always polite to refill the empty sake cup or glass of the other.

At parties in other countries, it is the host who offers wine to the guests but usually only once, after which it is up to the guests to help themselves. People of other countries may find the Japanese way to offering sake to be a little too persistent.

It may strike people of other countries as unnatural to see the Japanese at a Japanese-style dinner party stiffly standing on ceremony and pouring in a drink of sake to an important person.

However, at a dinner party held in a Japanese-style room, it is the custom for the guests to be seated to the right and left of the main guest in descending order of importance to form a square around the square room. Etiquette prescribes that paying respects to an important person requires getting up from one's seat and from the center of the room, proceeding so that one is positioned directly in front of the important person.

Question　**なぜ，日本ではバレンタイン・デーに女性が男性にチョコレートをあげるのですか？**

Answer　　　クリスチャンではないのに，クリスマスになるとクリスマス・ケーキを買って，家でクリスマス・パーティーをする日本人がいます。また，ほとんどの家で，子供にクリスマス・プレゼントをあげています。つまり，私たちは日本語にカタカナ語を取り入れるように，西洋の習慣も無条件に取り入れることができるのです。

　バレンタイン・デーは，3世紀ごろに殉教した聖バレンタインの祭日で，初めは親子の間で感謝の気持ちを書き記したカードを交換する習慣だったそうですが，20世紀になって，男女が愛を告白して贈り物をしたり，女性が男性に愛を告白する日にもなってきました。

　その習慣を商魂たくましく利用して，神戸の製菓会社モロゾフが，1936年，1952年と2度にわたって，この日に女性は好きな男性にチョコレートをあげよう，と宣伝を始めたのが，今の流行の最初です。1958年には東京の製菓会社もこの企画にのり，その後，一気に若い女性に人気の習慣となりました。

　1975年ごろ，2匹めのどじょうを狙って，ホワイト・デーなるものができ，1ヵ月後に，チョコレートをもらった男性が今度は女性にお返しをする，という習慣まで作ったのは余計なことでしたが——。

Q In Japan why is it the women the ones who give men chocolates on Valentine's Day?

A There are Japanese who are not Christians but who buy a Christmas cake to celebrate Christmas at home with a Christmas party. Nearly all Japanese families give their children Christmas presents on Christmas. In other words, the Japanese are unconditionally able to adopt Western customs, similar to the way they are unconditionally able to adopt English words into their language.

Valentine's Day began in the third century as a festival for the martyred St. Valentine. At first, the custom took on the form of parents and children exchanging cards with written messages that expressed gratitude.In the twentieth century, Valentine's Day became a day for both men and women to give presents to the other as a declaration of love, and also a day for the woman to declare her love to the man.

The Valentine's Day vogue of today had its beginnings in 1936 and 1952 when a Kobe confectionery, Morozoff, utilizing their shrewd commercialism in making the most of this custom, began a campaign calling on women to give chocolates to the man in their hearts. In 1958, another Tokyo confectionery took up this campaign and the custom became an instant hit among young women.

Around 1975, hoping that their luck would continue, White Day was conceived, which is a day coming one month after Valentine's Day where men give women whom they received chocolates from, chocolates back in return—which is really quite unnecessary.

Question　なぜ，日本では6月1日に，いっせいに夏服に かえるのですか？

Answer

　警官，デパートの女性店員，鉄道の職員，会社の事務の女性など，制服で仕事をしている人たちや，制服の学生たちは，6月1日に夏用の服にかえます。そして10月1日には再び，秋冬の服に戻ります。もちろん，そうすることが法律で決められているわけではありません。

　季節の変化がはっきりしている日本では，日本人は共通の季節感を持っていて，昔から季節の節目に衣服をかえることを習慣としていました。「衣替え」という言葉があるぐらいです。

　江戸時代には4月1日に夏の着物に，現代と同じように10月1日に冬の着物にかえていたそうです。その習慣が今でも私たちに残っているのです。

　制服は，その制服を着て仕事をしている集団が，社会と関わる上で必要な身分の表示となっているもので，そうだとすれば，いっせいにかえないと機能は発揮されません。

　自由な服装に慣れた帰国子女の人が，暑いからと，期日の前に着替えて学校に行ったら，イジメにあったという話もあります。これも文化摩擦の1つかもしれません。

Q. Why do the Japanese all change to summer wear on June 1?

A People who wear uniforms at work such as the police, salesclerks at department stores, railroad personnel, women office workers, and students who are required to wear school uniforms, all change to summer clothes on June 1. On October 1, they all change back to winter clothes. Of course, there is no law that requires this change to take place.

The Japanese have developed a mutual feel for the seasons living in a country with distinct changes in seasons. From old, it has been a custom to change to a different set of clothing at each new phase of the season. There is even a term, *koromogae*, or "to change to a different set of clothing at the turn of the seasons" to describe this change.

People in the Edo period (1600–1868) changed to summer kimono on April 1 and to winter kimono on October 1, the same day as the present. A vestige of this custom still prevails today.

Uniforms are a necessary indicator of the status of the group carrying out their work in society. The group's function will be obscured unless the change takes place at the same time by everyone.

One hears of students who have studied abroad and are used to dressing as they please. They go to school wearing summer clothes even before the designated date because of the heat and becoming the target of bullying. This may perhaps be one example of cultural friction.

Question なぜ, 日本では奥さんのことを「愚妻」と呼ぶのですか?

Answer
　　日本人が自分のこと, 自分の身内のことを謙遜して言うときに使う言葉の1つが「愚—」(おろかな)や,「拙—」(まずい, へたな)です。江戸時代に侍たちが, 自分のことを言うときに使っていた「拙者」という言葉も, ここから来ているわけです。

　　また最近はあまり使いませんが, 自分の息子のことを「豚児」と言ったり,「愚息」と言ったりもします。

　　日本人は不必要に自分を卑下することがあるということは, これまでもしばしば外国人から指摘されてきたことです。

　　外国人でも, 自分のことや自分の身内のことをあからさまにほめることはなく, 控えめに表現することは同じだと思いますが,「愚かな」といった語, 表現は用いないようですね。

　　日本人の精神の根底には, 謙虚であることが美徳の1つという考えがあり, 人に対して自己主張をしすぎたり, 自信たっぷりな態度は嫌われました。

　　従って, 人に対しては自分を控えめに見せると同時に, 自分の身内のことも控えめにしか言いません。人に話すときには,「うちの愚妻が——」, ということになるのです。今では, 夫がそんなことを言ったら, 奥さんに追い出されてしまうかもしれません。

Q Why do Japanese husbands call their wives *gusai* (my foolish wife)?

A *Gu* (foolish) is one of the humble forms used when the Japanese refer to themselves or to members of their family. Another humble form used is *setsu* meaning "bad" or "clumsy." *Sessha*, a term used during the Edo period (1600–1868) by the samurai to refer to themselves is derived from this form.

Although not often used nowadays, *tonji* and *gusoku*, with *ton* being the character for pig and *gu* being the character for foolish, both denote "my son."

It is frequently pointed out by people of other countries, that the Japanese sometimes unnecessarily disparage themselves.

Non-Japanese do not resort to all-out praise when referring to themselves or to members of their family. Like the Japanese, discretion is used but not to the point of referring to the other as "foolish."

Modesty is one of the virtues that forms the base of Japanese mentality. Being too haughty or too arrogant is frowned upon.

When talking to another, only through language such as "my foolish wife" can one lower the position of members of one's family and at the same time show one's modesty. But if a husband were to say this in this day and age, he would be thrown out of the house by his wife.

Question なぜ，日本のアパートでは犬，猫を飼っては いけないのですか？

Answer

　　日本で，マンションと言われる多層住宅がた くさん建築され始めたのは，1950年代の後半か らです。産業構造の変化に伴い，農村から人が都 会に流れ込み，都会の人口は急増しましたが，地 価の高騰で，都会に1戸建て住宅を取得すること が難しくなったため，マンションの人気が高ま っています。

　　しかし日本の場合，マンションの広さは決し て余裕のあるものではありません。1戸の広さは 50㎡から100㎡が大半です。

　　隣の家との間の防音も決して万全とは言え ず，けっこう隣や上下階の音が聞こえてきます。 そういうマンションに住む人の中には，当然，ペ ットは嫌い，という人も多く，キャンキャンと鳴 き声をあげる犬や，窓からニャーと訪問してく る猫は我慢なりません。

　　ただし，欧米でもNo petになっているアパー トはありますから，日本だけが特別というわけ ではないようです。

　　ペットを散歩させるときの，マンション周辺 の糞尿のトラブルも，あとを絶ちません。海外の 都市では，犬の散歩をするときに糞処理用のビ ニール袋やスコップを持って歩くのはまれで， 糞処理が市当局の悩みのタネになっているよう ですから，その点では日本の愛犬家のマナーの ほうが，まだ少しいいかもしれません。

Q Why can't Japanese keep dogs and/or cats in their condominiums?

A Many multi-storied dwellings such as condominiums began to be built in the latter 1950s. With the change in the industrial structure, people streamed into cities from the farming areas causing a sharp rise in the city population. Land prices skyrocketed and condominiums grew in popularity because of the difficulty in acquiring a single-family house.

However, condominiums in Japan cannot be said to be spacious. Most of the units are 50 m² to 100 m² (164 to 328 sq. ft.) in area.

Sound insulation between houses is inadequate and sound is easily carried from the neighboring houses as well as from the top and bottom units. This type of living arrangement is enough to make anyone dislike pets. They feel they need not put up with barking dogs or the meow of a visiting cat on a windowsill

This no-pet policy is not enforced solely in Japan. There are condominiums in the West too, that ban pets.

There is no end to the trouble caused by droppings left around the condominium area by pets being taken on a walk. In cities in other countries, it is rare to see animal owners carrying a plastic bag and a trowel to clean up after their pets, and this problem has continued to vex the city authorities. On this point, animal lovers in Japan may be the better rule observer.

Question　なぜ，日本のデパートや店は，日曜，祝日に休まないのですか？

Answer

　中国から移入された大陰太陽暦（旧暦）に基づいてできた日本の暦に，太陽暦が取り入れられたのは1873年のことです。そして，1876年4月1日には「官庁は，日曜を休日，土曜は半日休日にする」という通達が政府から出ます。

　日本ではそれまで，働く人たちの休日は，10日ごと，あるいは旧暦の1日と15日というのが普通でした。ですから官庁の休日の通達が出ても，一般社会では長く続いた習慣が一度に改まるわけはなく，昭和の初めまでは，政府の通達を横目に旧来の休みの習慣が根強く守られていました。

　今では日曜が休みというのは当然のことになりましたが，日本の日曜日は「安息日」という宗教上の慣習とは無縁ですから，休みである日曜日こそ，遊びに，買い物にと，人が繰り出すのは当然です。

　従って，デパートをはじめとした商店や遊園地などは，客をかき集めようと商魂をたくましくします。だからと言って，日本人が働きすぎているわけではなく，日曜日に働く人のためには，別の曜日に休みがあります。

Q Why don't department stores and other retail stores close on Sundays and holidays in Japan?

A Japan's calendar was formerly based on the old calendar, a cross between the lunar and solar calendars that was introduced from China. It was not until 1873 that Japan adopted the solar calendar. On April 1, 1876, the government issued an official notice declaring Sunday a holiday and Saturday a half-day for all governmental offices.

Until then, Japanese workers took days off every ten days or on the first and fifteenth of every month according to the lunar calendar. Although an official notice was issued from the goverment office concerning holidays, the people held fast to their former practice of taking days off and were not quick to adopt to the new system. It was not until the beginning of the Showa period (1926–89) that changes began to take place.

Taking Sundays off has now become widely accepted. Because of religious differences, the Sabbath as a day of rest is not religiousiy significant to the Japanese, and this day is invariably spent doing other things such as shopping and enjoying a pastime.

Department stores and amusement parks vie for customers, but this is not to say that the Japanese are workaholics. An alternate day off is given to people who work on Sundays.

Question なぜ，日本の家ではトイレでスリッパを履きかえるのですか？

Answer

　　明治・大正生まれのお年寄りの中には，トイレのことを「御不浄」と言う人がいます。この日本語は「きれいでない，汚れている」ということを意味します。

　　昔は，大小便は便壺に溜め，一杯になったら汲み出す，というのが日本のトイレの一般的な姿でした。ですから臭うのです，強烈に！　蛆もわいたし，金蠅も来るし，確かに汚いところであったのです。

　　従って，昔の一般の日本家屋では，トイレが屋内にあることはなく，少し離れた所に造るのが普通で，履物を履いてトイレに行きました。建物の一部になっていても，居間などから最も遠いところに，渡り廊下などでちょっと離した形で造ってありました。

　　しかし，20世紀の後半になって，主な都市で下水道が整うと共に，日本の家にも水洗トイレが普及していきます。水洗ですから衛生上の問題も全くなくなります。

　　しかし，トイレが「御不浄」であったという観念は，私たち日本人の頭からなかなか抜けません。畳の上を歩いた素足や，居間の床の上を歩いたスリッパのままトイレに入るのは，やはり抵抗があるのです。そこで，なぜかトイレ専用スリッパが存在する次第です。

Q Why do the Japanese change to a different pair of slippers when using the lavatory?

A Some of the elderly, born during the Meiji (1868– 1912) and Taisho periods (1912–26) sometimes refer to the lavatory as *gofujou*, or "filthy."

Lavatories in Japan were formerly a large opening into which feces and urine were deposited. The contents were then pumped out when full. The smell was awful and unbearable! It was indeed filthy—full of maggots and attracting large, greenbottle flies.

In the past, lavatories were not built in Japanese houses but built a short distance away from the house. Slippers were worn to where the lavatory was located. Although it was a part of the structure of the house, it was built so that it was separated by a corridor and located the farthest possible distance away from the living room.

The latter half of the twentieth century saw the improvement of the sewage system in major cities and flush toilets became commonplace in many homes. There are now no problems regarding sanitation with flush toilets.

However, the concept that lavatories are filthy is still entrenched in the Japanese mind. They are not used to the idea of entering a lavatory after walking across a tatami mat with bare feet, or with slippers used to walk across the floor of the living room with. And for this reason, slippers exist for exclusive lavatory use even today.

Question　なぜ,日本人は新幹線や飛行機の中で靴を脱ぐのですか?

Answer

　　日本の格式の高いホテルの廊下で,スリッパで歩いている人を,ごくたまにですが見掛けることがあります。ベッドに入る以外には靴を脱がない欧米人にとっては,靴を脱いでホテルの廊下を歩くということは,洋服を脱いで歩いているのと同じくらいショッキングなシーンとして映るそうですが,本当でしょうか。

　　逆に多くの日本人にとっては,和風の家である以上,自分の家ではもちろん,よその家に行っても靴を脱ぐのがあたりまえですから,新幹線や飛行機の中で靴を脱ぐことにも,なんの抵抗感もありません。

　　それに,日本の庶民が靴を履き始めたのは明治以降のことですから,明治維新から100年たったとはいえ,まだまだ靴が足に「馴染んで」いなくて,靴を脱がないとくつろげないのかもしれません。

　　このため,日本の航空会社の中には,乗客にスリッパをプレゼントしているところもあります。欧米人でもそれを利用している人がけっこういますから,「郷に入れば,郷に従え」で,外国人も靴を脱いでくつろげばいいのではないでしょうか。

Q Why do the Japanese take off their shoes on the *shinkansen* and airplanes?

A People can occasionally be seen wearing slippers and walking along the hallways of posh Japanese hotels. Is it true that Westerners, who do not take off their shoes except when going to bed, find walking in the hallways without shoes to be equally shocking as walking without clothes?

On the other hand, many Japanese feel it is only proper to remove their shoes in Japanese-style homes—when entering the homes of others not to mention their own home; hence, they have no qualms about removing their shoes on the *shinkansen* and airplane.

It was only from the Meiji period (1868–1912) onward that shoes began to be worn by the common people and although one hundred years have already elapsed since the Meiji Restoration, perhaps shoes not yet having adjusted to the feet may be the reason behind the Japanese not being able to relax unless the shoes are removed.

There are some Japanese airline companies that offer slippers to their passengers as a gift and there are many Westerners who make use of these slippers. Like the proverb, "When in Rome do as the Romans do," perhaps this is not a bad idea after all.

Question　なぜ, もっと着物を着ないのですか?

Answer

　　動きやすい, 1日じゅう着ていても着くずれが
しない, 上下の自由な組み合わせができる, 暑さ,
寒さに対応しやすい——などなど, 洋服の利点
は着物に比べて圧倒的です。

　　しかし, 結婚式など改まった時には, 今でも着
物を着ることがあるわけですから, もう少しふ
だんから着物を着てもいいのかもしれません。

　　ところが難点があります。慣れないと着付け
が実に厄介なのです。今時, 自分で着物をきちん
と着ることができる若い人はほとんどいませ
ん。お母さんや美容室の着付けの人の世話にな
らなければ着ることができません。しかし, 最近
のお母さん自体も, 自分で着物を着ることがで
きない世代になってきています。

　　それに着物の手入れが面倒です。合成繊維で,
そのままクリーニングに出せるものもあります
が, 高級なものは洗い張りといって, 特別の洗濯
法が必要で, 費用もかかります。

　　さらにもう1つ。着物を若い人が敬遠する理由
に, 下着の問題もあります。ふだんと同じパンティー
ーをはいて着物を着ると, 着物にパンティー
の線が出てしまうし, トイレに行ったときにも
実に不便です。裾をまくった後の着付けも乱れ
て整えるのが大変になります。とにかく現代人
には疲れる衣服なのです。

Q Why isn't the kimono worn more often?

A The benefits of wearing Western clothes compared to the kimono are many. Western clothes can be worn the whole day without coming loose, the top and bottom can be freely matched, it can be easily adapted to heat and cold, etc.

The kimono however, is worn even today at weddings and on formal occasions, so perhaps wearing a kimono regularly would not be such a bad idea after all.

But there are drawbacks. Wearing a kimono properly can be troublesome unless one is used to wearing one. There are very few people in the younger generation nowadays who are able to wear a kimono properly. They have to depend on their mothers or pay more than 10,000 yen (US $90) to have a beauty shop consultant help them. However, the mothers are now of the generation where they themselves are unable to wear a kimono properly.

The care that must go into a kimono can be a burden. Those made of synthetic fibers can be dry cleaned, but high quality kimonos must be cleaned by *araihari*, a special process that is costly.

Another reason why the younger people shun the kimono is the problem of underwear. Regular panties cannot be worn with a kimono because the contour shows up clearly under the kimono. Using the lavatory is a great inconvenience. The kimono comes loose when the skirt of the kimono is pulled up, and straightening it out is a big hassle. At any rate, wearing a kimono is just too much of a headache for the contemporary person.

Question　なぜ，日本では図書館よりも書店が多いのですか？

Answer　　一般市民のための図書館の数は，その国の文化のバロメーターとも言われますから，その点からすれば日本は文化の後進国で，図書館の数が少なすぎます。

　イギリスではすでに1850年に図書館法が成立し，税金でまかなわれる無料公開の市民のための図書館が次々と設立され，アメリカでも19世紀のうちに公共図書館は数を増やしていったのです。

　ところが，日本で図書館法が成立したのは1950年のことでした。欧米におくれること約100年。今や公共図書館は着々と増えつつあり，1985年には1633館だったものが，1995年では2297館になっていますが，欧米に比べればまだまだ貧弱です。

　一方，1995年4月段階で，日本書店組合連合会に加入している書店は1万967店。加入していない書店を合わせると約2万店と言われます。図書館が普及してきたからといって，書店の数が減ったというわけではなく，図書館が果たせない役割——新しい情報の提供，マンガ・大衆小説などの娯楽，学習参考書などの提供は，書店が受け持っているのが現状です。

Q Why are there more bookstores than libraries in Japan?

A The number of libraries available to the general public is said to be a barometer of the country's culture, and on this point, Japan is a backward country because there are too few libraries.

The Library Law enacted in England in 1850 established free libraries open to the public covered by taxes. The United States increased its number of public libraries in the nineteenth century.

Japan enacted the Library Law in 1950, one hundred years after the West. The number of public libraries has been steadily increasing and while there were 1,633 libraries in 1985, it increased to 2,297 in 1995 but even then, Japan still lags far behind the West.

Bookstores that are members of the Federation of Japan Bookstores as of April 1995 numbered 10,967. Including bookstores that are not members, the overall number of bookstores is approximately 20,000. The number of bookstores has not decreased with the spread of libraries. Bookstores fulfill a role not covered by libraries such as: providing up-to-date information, providing reading matter for entertainment such as comics and popular novels, and providing study reference materials.

Question なぜ, 喫茶店のコーヒー1杯の値段があんなに高いのですか?

Answer

　今, 町中のちょっとした喫茶店のコーヒーの値段は, 400円ぐらいのようです。このうち原価なんてたかがしれています。ところが, この値段が繁華街にある店では800円とか, 1000円とかになることもあるのです。

　つまり, 日本ではコーヒーに限らず, 喫茶店の飲み物などの値段は, 飲食物そのものの値段と考えてはいけません。ひとときの休憩をする場所代と考えてください。

　コーヒーの原価から計算すれば, 日本全国どこでもそうは変わらないはずですが, それぞれの喫茶店がある土地の価格となると, 場所によって天地の差があります。店の家賃がグンと高いわけですから, 経営者としては, 店の雰囲気をぐっと高級にしたりすることによって, また, コーヒーの入れ方にも凝ったりして料金を高くし, 場所代を捻出しようとするわけです。

Q Why is a cup of coffee at coffee shops so expensive?

A Although the actual cost of producing coffee is negligible, a regular cup of coffee at a coffee shop now costs about 400 yen (US $3.50). In a busy section of town, the price can go up as high as 800 yen (US $7.15) or even to 1,000 yen (US $8.90).

Not only coffee, but prices of drinks at coffee shops should not be regarded as just drinks per se. It should be regarded as a location charge covering the cost of enjoying a short break.

The actual price of a cup of coffee does not differ appreciably throughout Japan, but location makes all the difference in price considering that the cost of land of the various coffee shops vary. If the rent is high, the coffee shop owner attempts to devise means to raise the price of a cup of coffee to cover the high rent such as bringing elegance and luxuriousness into the overall atmosphere of the coffee shop, or choosing to be particular about how the coffee is made and served to bring out the best in coffee.

Question なぜ，日本では年末になるとベートーベンの
第九交響曲をやるのですか？

Answer 　年末恒例の音楽会になってきたのは，1970年
ごろからです。

　この曲は合唱付きと言われるもので，フル・オ
ーケストラを前にして4人の独唱者，そして大合
唱団が並ぶ，曲も演奏風景も壮大な交響曲です。
特に合唱部分は，日本人で知らない人はいませ
ん。クラシックのファンにはこたえられない曲
ですが，大掛かりですので，欧米では演奏される
回数は決して多くはないようです。

　しかしこの曲が，1年の終わりに近くなり気持
ちの上でも，また町中の雰囲気にしても，なんと
なく騒然としてくる日本には，なぜかぴったり
とくるのです。

　そこで，日本国内にも多くの交響楽団が誕生
してくるにつれ，日本のあちこちで第九の演奏
会が開かれるようになってきました。特に，オー
ケストラの楽団員のボーナスをひねり出すため
にも必要な演奏会になったのです。

　さらに，お祭り好きの日本人は，聴くだけでは
なく，合唱団の一員として参加することが夢と
なっていきます。そして，日本全国で各地域のア
マチュア合唱団が，続々とこの曲の演奏会を企
画するようになりました。

　入場料の収益の一部はチャリティーにするな
ど，名目も十分で，日本では，第九がないと年末
の気分にならなくなってしまいました。

Q Why is Beethoven's Symphony No.9 played at the end of the year?

A Beethoven's Symphony No.9 performed as a year-end concert has become an annual event since around 1970.

Said to be a symphony with a chorus, it is performed with a full orchestra with four vocal soloists and a large choir. It is a magnificent symphony both in music and in the grandeur of the sight. There is no Japanese who is not familiar with the chorus part of the symphony. The music deeply affects classical music fans, but because it is such a large-scale undertaking, it is not performed very often in the West.

This piece ties in nicely with a kind of a pervasive restlessness felt throughout the country stemming from the year coming to an end and the bustling mood in the city.

The ninth is performed in a variety of places as more and more symphony orchestras are formed throughout Japan. Holding this concert has become an indispensable means of raising funds to pay for the musicians' year-end bonus.

The festival-loving Japanese are not content just to listen to the ninth. Many dream of singing as a member of the choir. Non-professional choirs throughout Japan in succession plan concerts to perform the ninth.

The ninth can be held on a number of pretexts such as using a portion of the proceeds for charity. There are now many people who feel something amiss with the year-end mood without hearing the ninth.

Question なぜ，日本の店ではりっぱな包装をするのですか？

Answer

　日本の包装の歴史は古く，すでに原始時代に木の葉，竹の皮，また織物でも包装された証拠が残っています。

　正倉院の宝物の中には，シルクロードを通って運ばれてきたガラス製品などもありますが，おそらく壊れないように優れた包装が施されていたに違いありません。伎楽面(ぎがくめん)を包んだ大きい風呂敷も残っています。

　江戸時代の1764年には，『包結図説』という本が出て，礼法に基づく様々な包み方，結び方が紹介されていることからもわかるように，「包む」ということは日本人の古来の美意識に育てられてきたものです。「折る」「たたむ」「結ぶ」というのが日本の包装の基本です。

　京都や奈良の老舗(しにせ)は古くから包装を競いあっていましたし，その伝統が現代まで長く続いています。そして，包装紙のデザイン自体が一種のブランドとなっています。

　品物の形に合わせて包むという包装の仕方は西洋風の包み方で，デパートなどがサービスとして取り入れましたが，比較的に手間がかかることから，過剰サービスという声もあります。今では袋に入れてしまうことが多くなってきたようです。しかし，手なれた人の包装は実に見事で，日本人は手先が器用だということを証明しています。

Q Why are purchases wrapped so nicely at stores in Japan?

A The history of wrapping in Japan goes way back to the primitive age where there is evidence that bark of trees, sheaths of bamboo shoots and fabrics were used as wrapping.

Treasures at the Shosoin Temple include glass manufactured articles that came by way of the Silk Road. They were undoubtedly carefully wrapped to prevent breakage. A large *furoshiki* (wrapping cloth) used to wrap a *gigaku* (an ancient masked dance) mask is also kept there.

It is now known from the various ways of wrapping and tying based on etiquette depicted in the book, *Hōketsu-zusetsu* (An Illustrated Guide to Wrapping) printed in 1764 in the Edo period (1600–1868), that wrapping had grown into the time-honored Japanese sense of the artistic. The basics of wrapping are bending, folding and tying.

Long established stores in Kyoto and Nara have continued to vie with each other in the art of wrapping and this tradition has endured to the present day. The designs on the wrapping paper itself is a type of a unique brand.

Wrapping to fit the shape of the article is a Western style of wrapping that Japanese department stores have adopted as a service to their customers, but there are people who regard this as excessive service because of the amount of time and trouble that go into it. Now, purchases are oftentimes simply put into a bag. The neatness in the way an article is wrapped by a skillful person is truly superb, evidence of the dexterousness of the Japanese.

**Question　なぜ，日本では「車は左，人は右」の通行に
なっているのですか？**

Answer

　　日本は1967年に「道路交通条約」(Convention
on Road Traffic)という国際条約に加入していま
すが，その条約の加盟国では，車両は左側通行に
なっています。

　　1872年に新橋―品川間の鉄道敷設以来，次々
と建設されていく鉄道は，2車線の場合，イギリ
スの方式に従って，すでに左側走行にされてい
ましたし，自動車も左側走行が慣習となってい
ました。アメリカでは車両は右側通行ですから，
日本に来た多くのアメリカ人はまごつきます
が，世界には左側走行の国もけっこう多いので
す。

　　「車は左，人は右」という現在の日本の交通規
則は，1949年5月20日に制定されました。「人は
右」と決まったのは，車が左側通行ですから，向
かい合って歩いたほうが危険を避けられる，と
いうのが理由だそうです。しかし，どうも人間に
は左側を歩く習性があるのではないでしょうか。

　　一般に，日本人に限らず，世の中には右利きの
人が多く，利き腕を自由に使えるように左側に
寄って歩くのだ，というのが理由かもしれませ
ん。

Q Why do cars keep to the left side of the street and pedestrians to the right?

A Japan joined the Convention on Road Traffic in 1967 in which vehicles of all member nations were driven on the left hand side of the road.

Railroads were being laid one after another since the laying of the railroad between Shimbashi and Shinagawa in 1872 and when comprised of two tracks, they were already being driven on the left side following the British system. Even cars were driven on the left side of the street. Vehicles drive on the right in the U.S. and there are many Americans who are thrown into confusion when they come to Japan, but there are many countries where vehicles are driven on the left side of the street.

The present traffic rule in Japan of assigning people to the right and cars to the left was enacted on May 20, 1949. The "people to the right" rule was designated because vehicular traffic ran on the left side of the street and it was assumed that walking when facing traffic would minimize the danger of accidents occurring. However, human beings seem to have an inclination to walk on the left side.

However, the reason may simply be that there are more right-handed people than left-handed people not only in Japan but throughout the world. Walking on the left side leaves the dominant hand free with ample room to move freely.

2

日本人の
マナーと行動の
ふしぎ

Puzzling Manners and
Behavior of
the Japanese

Question　なぜ，日本には外で立ち小便をする男の人が多いのですか？

Answer

　昔，ヴェルサイユ宮殿にはトイレがなく，庭やとびらなどの物陰でしたそうですが，世界中どこでも，排泄に関する感覚はおおらかだったように思えます。

　日本でも同様で，京都には，江戸時代まで道の側に桶が置いてあって，道行く人はそこで平気で排泄をしたといいます。女性も利用していて，その風景は，江戸から来た人には京の名物になっていたそうです。

　しかし今では，公衆トイレが整備されてきていますし，法律でも立ち小便は罰せられるようになっていますから，公然と立ち小便をする人はいないはずです。

　確かに，飲みすぎたビールを電柱の陰や路地で放出する人がいますが，あえて同情して言えば，日本の街がいかにも狭すぎるのが不運です。特に，狭い地域に飲食店が立ち並ぶ繁華街では，尿意を催しても人目を避けるところがなく，ついたまりかねて──となったら外国人でもそこらでやりませんか？

Q Why do many men urinate in the open in Japan?

A Long ago, there were no lavatories at the Palace of Versailles so people did it in the garden or behind objects like doors. The concept of elimination of bodily wastes was rather liberal throughout the world.

In Japan also, it is said that up to the Edo period (1600–1868) in Kyoto, buckets were placed along both sides of the road for the convenience of passersby who would nonchalantly use them when the urge came. The buckets were also used by women. This scene was hailed as Kyoto's special feature by people from Tokyo.

In present day Japan however, public lavatories are available everywhere. There is also a law banning urinating in the streets, so there is probably no one who would do it in the open.

Of course, there are those who drink too much beer and resort to doing it behind telephone and electric light poles or in alleys. If a stance may be taken on their side, it is indeed unfortunate that the streets and town area in Japan are so narrow and confining. When the urge to go strikes, especially in a cramped area in a busy section of town where clubs, bars, and eating places serving food and drinks all stand in a row, and there is no place where one could possibly be inconspicuous, and one has to go—wouldn't even people from other countries do it?

Question なぜ，日本では歩きながら物を食べてはいけないのですか？

Answer

　　日本の食事は座って，そして，器に盛った食べ物を箸を使って食べるのが基本です。箸は中国から伝来し，奈良時代にはすでに2本の箸の使用が一般化していました。

　　欧米ではテーブルに着いてフォーク，ナイフ，スプーンを用いて食べることが基本でしょうが，違うのはパンを手に取って食べることです。ちゃんとしたフランス料理店でも，パンだけはテーブル・クロスの上にポンと置いて，パンくずを散らかして食べるのが，日本人にはどうもなじめません。

　　サンドイッチ，ホットドッグ，ハンバーガーなどは，もう，手でつかまないかぎり食べられないようにできている食べ物ですね。それに比べて，一般的な日本の食事では，主食の御飯をはじめとして，手で食べるものはありません。

　　外で食べることができるように工夫された握り飯などはありますし，また，夜店で買った食べ物を歩きながら食べることもあるでしょうが，それは限られた場合のことです。

　　従って日本では必然的に，食べ物を手づかみで食べることや，まして，歩きながら食べるのはマナーが悪いことになってしまいました。しかし，日本でも街頭にスナックの店が立ち並ぶようになりましたし，今の若い人たちは，歩きながら食べることにあまり抵抗はないようです。

Q Why don't people in Japan eat while walking?

A Table manners in Japan dictate that one is to sit and eat food served in dishes with chopsticks. Chopsticks were introduced into Japan from China, and by the Nara period (710–794), using chopsticks as a pair was the accepted way of eating.

Table manners in the West also, require one to sit and eat using forks, knives and spoons. One difference, however, is that bread is eaten with the hands. At French-style restaurants, bread is simply placed on the tablecloth and picked up and eaten as bread crumbs fly. The Japanese are not accustomed to eating this way.

Sandwiches, hot dogs, hamburgers, etc. are made so that they cannot be eaten unless picked up with the hands. In comparison, Japanese food in general, even its staple food rice, cannot be eaten with the hands.

Rice balls devised for outdoor eating and food bought at night stalls can be eaten while walking but these are exceptions.

It was an inevitable consequence that eating with the hands and much more so, eating while walking was regarded as bad manners. However, now that many concession stands have sprung up in Japan, there are many youths who are very open about eating while walking.

Question　なぜ，日本の女性は笑うときに手で口を隠すのですか？

Answer

　　古来，日本女性の礼儀の1つとして，人前で歯をむきだして笑わない，大口を開けて口の中を見せない，ということがあります。

　　厳しくそう言われてきた理由の1つとして，昔，日本では女性がお歯黒といって，歯を黒く染めていたことが挙げられます。

　　お歯黒という習慣は，奈良時代（710—794）以前からある風習で，平安時代（794—1185）には貴族の女性の間で盛んでした。平安時代後期には，公家，武家の男性も行っています。室町時代（1333—1568）には，女子が9歳になると歯を染めて成人の印としています。その後，江戸時代（1600—1868）に入ると結婚した女性はすべてお歯黒にしています。

　　鉄片を茶や酢に浸して酸化させた液を歯に塗って黒くするのですが，黒い歯を剥き出しにするのをためらって，笑うときは着物の袖や手で口許を覆うことが，女性の上品さを保つための礼儀作法とされてきたわけです。

　　外国人は，日本女性が口元を隠して笑うこのしぐさに，幼児性を感じるのだそうです。確かに，心理学者フロイトが，笑うときに口を隠すのは幼児の習性だと言っています。

　　しかし，年配の人はともかく，現代の若い女性は口元に手を当てて笑うことはありませんね。

Q Why do Japanese women cover their mouth with their hand when they laugh?

A From way back, not baring one's teeth in front of others when laughing and not opening one's mouth wide and showing the inside of the mouth was one of the decorums of etiquette strictly observed by women.

It was strictly observed because from ancient times, women in Japan dyed their teeth black (*ohaguro*).

The custom of *ohaguro* began during the Nara period (710–794) onward and it became popular among the aristocratic women in the Heian period (794–1185). In the latter Heian, it was also practiced by men court nobles and the samurai. During the Muromachi period (1333–1568), girls who reached nine years of age dyed their teeth as a mark of having attained adulthood. During the Edo period (1600–1868), all married women dyed their teeth.

The black color was derived from soaking a piece of iron that was left to oxidize in a liquid of tea and vinegar. Hesitant about showing their blackened teeth, women hid their mouth with their hand or kimono sleeve. This was considered to be an act of courtesy that reflected refinement.

Non-Japanese seem to feel that covering the mouth when laughing is a sign of immaturity on the part of Japanese women. And indeed, the psychiatrist Freud has said that covering the mouth while laughing is an exhibition of infantile behavior.

Excluding elderly women, there are very few young women of today who cover their mouth when laughing.

Question　**なぜ，日本人はせかせかと食事をするのですか？**

Answer　　日本の武士の世界に「早飯，早糞，早支度」という言葉がありました。戦いに備えた武士の心構えであったわけです。その伝統は，日本の軍隊の世界にも引き継がれていたようで，やはり忙しい食事だったそうです。

　従って，日本人は食事を短時間にとることに抵抗がなかったし，むしろ奨励されていました。

　今は時代が違ったとはいえ，今度は武士に代わって忙しいビジネス戦士が慌ただしい食事をしています。これは日本もアメリカも同様です。

　日本の多くの会社の昼休みは，12時から1時までが原則です。ヨーロッパのいくつかの国々のように，2時間，3時間などということはありません。しかも，いっせいに昼休みになるのですから，出遅れると，食堂や売店の前で列を作って待たなければならなくなります。なんとか昼食にありついても，順番を待っている人たちのために，早く席を空けてあげなければなりません。

　朝は朝で，ぎりぎりに起きて，大急ぎで朝食をとり，長時間の通勤電車に飛び乗らねばなりませんし，夜は残業で，落ち着いて夕食を取る時間もないというわけです。

　子供は，となると，食事をさっと済ませて，塾や習い事に駆け回るというわけですから，小さいときからゆっくり食事をとる習慣ができていないのかもしれません。

Q Why do the Japanese eat so fast?

A There is a saying in samurai tradition that mentally prepared the samurai warrior for war: "eat fast, defecate quickly and dress quickly." This tradition seemed to have carried over to the Japanese military where meals were said to have been consumed in a hurry.

The Japanese see nothing wrong with eating their meals in a short period of time and are encouraged to do so.

Although not of the same time period, busy corporate warriors of today eat their meals in a hurry. This applies in Japan as well as in the United States.

Lunch hour in many Japanese companies usually runs from twelve to one. There is no two-hour or three-hour break as seen in some European countries. All companies generally follow the same lunch hour, so leaving the company late for lunch will result in a long wait in line at restaurants and at eating stands. Managing to get a seat or a bite to eat somewhere is no cause to linger over lunch. One cannot afford to spend too much time over lunch for the benefit of those waiting their turn in line.

Mornings are spent waking up at the last minute, gobbling down breakfast, and rushing off to catch the train for a long commute to work. Evenings are spent working until late leaving no time to eat dinner leisurely.

The children eat quickly and rush off to cram school or to some lesson. They have no time to develop a habit when little of taking their time over meals.

Question　なぜ，食べるときに音を立てるのですか？

Answer

　　日本語には「舌鼓を打つ」という表現があります。おいしいものを食べるときに，舌で音を立てて食べる様子を表した表現です。英語のsmack one's lipsと似ています。

　　日本の食事でも当然，不必要にクチャクチャと音を立てることは下品ですが，上品においしそうに食べているのであれば，少々の音を立てても，だれも咎める人はいません。

　　第一，日本の食事はどうしても音が出るようになっています。それは，熱くないとおいしくないものがあるからです。

　　特に，味噌汁などの汁物はできたてが最高ですが，熱いですから，どうしても空気といっしょに音を立てて，すすらなければなりません。鍋物も同様。てんぷらも揚げたてのアツアツが最高です。

　　洋食のスープは少々熱くても，スプーンで口元に持ってくるまでには適度に冷め，音を立てなくても飲むことができます。

　　それにお蕎麦。蕎麦の食べ方には1つのファッションがあって，音を立ててズルズルと口に入れ，かまないでのどにぐいと呑み込むのが，粋だと言われています。

　　洋食は洋食のルールで，和食は和食のルールで食べればいいのです。

Q Why do the Japanese slurp when eating?

A There is an expression in Japanese, *shita zutsumi wo utsu*, or, to smack one's lips when eating something good. Making a sound when eating something with relish is apparently the same in Japanese as in English.

Although making unnecessary noises when eating is considered rude even in Japan, enjoying something with gusto while observing good manners is no cause for rebuke.

In the first place, Japanese food is made for slurping because there are certain foods that must be piping hot in order to be enjoyed.

Soup such as miso soup, especially, is best when just made. Because it is very hot, the lips must be brought in direct contact with the bowl and the contents consumed together with air, causing one to slurp. This goes for *nabe-mono*, a hot pot cooked at the table. And piping-hot, just fried tempura is something not to be missed!

Western-style soup is also hot, but a spoon is used and an appropriate temperature is reached by the time the soup is brought to the mouth. There is no need to slurp.

And there is also soba. There is a certain style to follow when eating *soba*. It should first be slurped noisily into the mouth, then shoveled all the way to the back of the throat and swallowed down with a gulp. This is the chic way.

Western foods should be eaten following rules applied to Western food and Japanese food should be eaten following rules applied to Japanese food.

Question　なぜ，自分を指すときに鼻の頭を指すのですか？

Answer

　日本人がなぜ鼻を指して自分のことを示すのか，はっきりした理由はわかりません。同様に，自分を示すときに掌で自分の胸を押さえるようにするのはなぜかという問いに，欧米人も明確な答えを出せないのではないでしょうか。

　しかし，少なくとも，日本人と英米人との鼻についての意識の違いが，ジェスチャーの違いを生み出しているようでもあります。

　英語で，look down one's nose，また turn up one's nose，make a long nose などというと，「人を軽蔑する」という意味だそうですから，鼻は人に失礼な表現をイメージさせる存在のようです。鼻の前で掌を立ててひらひらさせると，相手を馬鹿にするしぐさになるそうですし——。

　日本語で「鼻が高い」というと「誇らしい」という意味ですし，顔の中心にある鼻は，誇りの象徴として考えられているふしがあります。日本語にも「鼻であしらう」（＝馬鹿にする，軽くみる），「鼻にかける」（＝得意がる）などの表現もありますが，英米よりは，鼻が相手に与える印象は不快ではないようです。

　近世まで，自分のことを言うのに「鼻様」という言葉があったそうで，これは鼻を指して自分のことを言うことから来たそうです。

Q Why do the Japanese point to their nose when referring to themselves?

A There is no clear answer as to why the Japanese point to their nose when referring to themselves. Westerners also, probably cannot give a clear answer as to why they refer to themselves by placing the palm of their hand on their chest.

The differences in gestures may have arisen from the differences in the way the Japanese, American, and English perceive the nose

"Nose" appearing in idioms such as "look down one's nose," "turn up one's nose," and "to make a long nose" all carry a derogatory meaning in English and hence, nose has taken on an image that connotes rudeness. Standing the palm of the hand and fluttering it on the nose indicates contempt for the other.

Because it is located in the center of the face, nose in Japan was taken in the context of symbolizing pride as in the expression, *hana ga takai* meaning "to be proud of." There are also other expressions such as *hana de ashirau* meaning "to treat a person with contempt" or "to look down on a person," and *hana ni kakeru* meaning "to boast of." But there are not nearly as many offensive expressions concerning the nose in Japanese as there are in English.

Until recent times, the expression *hana sama* used for oneself was derived from pointing to the nose to refer to oneself.

Question なぜ，日本人は電車の中でよく眠るのですか？

Answer

　以前はサラリーマンが主でしたが，最近は若い連中もよく眠っています。その一番の理由は，特に都会における過酷な通勤，通学時間の長さでしょう。なにしろ東京や大阪などの大都会では勤め先や学校が遠くなり，通勤，通学に1時間以上ということが珍しくないのです。

　サラリーマンの平均的睡眠時間は7時間を切っており，働き過ぎのサラリーマンや受験勉強に追われている学生たちは，常に慢性的な睡眠不足の状態であり，電車の中は恰好の憩いの場所となるわけです。

　日本の電車の中は，冬は暖房，夏は冷房という至れり尽くせりで，特に冬，座席の下から出てくる暖かい空気は人の眠気を誘います。

　会社の帰りに一杯ひっかけて，ほろ酔い機嫌で帰る時ともなると，これまた，座ったとたんにグースカとなるのも必然です。

　日本の電車の中の治安のよさも，安心した眠りができる理由でもあります。最近は少々物騒にはなりましたが，仮にぐっすり寝込んでも，バッグや財布を盗まれたりすることは，めったにないのが日本なのです。

　また，日本人がよく眠るのは，炭水化物が多い日本の食事が原因だとも言われています。消化に時間がかかり眠気を誘うからです。

Q Why do Japanese often sleep on trains?

A Until recently, people who slept on trains were mostly businessmen, but the younger people now have also begun to sleep on trains. This is due in large part, especially in the cities, to the grueling and long commute to work and to school. A commuting time of an hour or more one way is not uncommon in large cities such as Tokyo and Osaka where one's place of work or school is often located quite a distance away.

Businessmen get on the average, less than seven hours of sleep a night. The train becomes a most suitable place to rest for overworked businessmen and students cramming for exams, both who suffer from chronic lack of sleep.

It is the perfect place with heating in the winter and air-conditioning in the summer. Heat coming out from under the seats in winter is enough to make anyone feel drowsy.

Stopping for a drink after work and returning home slightly intoxicated inevitably causes one to fall asleep on the train the minute one hits the seat.

The safety of Japanese trains is another reason that can be cited why people can fall asleep feeling safe and secure. Although it has become a little unsafe now, bags and wallets are rarely stolen from slumbering passengers.

Also the large intake of carbohydrates in the Japanese diet makes the Japanese fall asleep on trains. It takes a little longer to digest carbohydrates which brings about drowsiness.

Question　なぜ，話すときに相手の目を見ないのですか？

Answer

　日本では確かに，一般的な礼儀として，相手の胸元ぐらいを見て話すほうが，穏やかな印象で，相手にこちらの話を聞こうとする気持ちにさせる，と言われてきました。

　自分よりも年齢や身分が高い人を「目上の人」，つまり「自分の目の上にいる人」と表現するぐらいですから，対等に目を合わせることは失礼だとさえ思われていました。

　欧米では相手の目を見て話すことには，もっと積極的な意味があり，1つは「あなたを信用しています」という意思の表示，もう1つは「私は本心を話しています，信じてください」というアピールだそうですから，目を見つめて話さない日本人に，欧米人が面食らうのはよくわかります。

　しかし今では日本でも，自分の意思を相手にきちんと伝えようとするときは，相手の目を見て話すようにと，親からも，学校でも教えられていますから，海外で活躍する日本人も含めて，多くの日本人が，欧米人とでも，また日本人同士でも，目をそらさずに堂々と話をするようになっていると思います。

　一般的に言えば，「恐れいりますが――」という言葉に象徴されるように，相手を優位に置いて関係の和を保とうとする日本人の心理から，まだまだ，一歩引いた感じで相手の目を見ているところがあるのが現状でしょうか――。

Q Why don't the Japanese look the other person in the eye when speaking?

A Etiquette prescribes that fixing one's eyes on the chest of the other when speaking leads to a better impression and instills in the other a desire to hear what one has to say.

An expression referring to a person who is older or of a higher rank than oneself is, *meue no hito* meaning a person who is above one's eyes. For this reason, the Japanese considered it rude to meet the gaze of the other on equal terms.

For Westerners, establishing eye contact when speaking is looked upon as positive, meaning "I trust you" and it is also an appeal to the other meaning, "I'm speaking from the bottom of my heart. Please trust me." Westerners may find the Japanese avoidance of eye contact to be baffling.

Parents and schools nowadays teach children the importance of establishing eye contact when speaking to convey intent. Many Japanese now, including those who are active in establishing themselves abroad, are able to speak confidently with Westerners and with other Japanese with eye contact.

Generally speaking, the expression, *osoreirimasu ga—* meaning "I am very sorry to—" symbolizes the psychology of the Japanese in placing the other in a superior position to maintain a harmonious relationship. Although eye contact is established, the Japanese still tend to put the other person on a higher footing than themselves.

Question　なぜ，もらったプレゼントを人前で開けないのですか？

Answer

　アメリカ映画を見ていると，プレゼントをもらった人が，すぐに包装をバリバリと破いて中の物を取り出してしまうシーンが出てきます。クリスマスの包装など，きれいな紙が使われているのに平気で破きます。そんなシーンを見ると，多くの日本人は「きれいな包装をあんなに無神経に破って──」と思ってしまいます。

　日本では折り紙，のし袋，また，最近は使う人が少なくなった風呂敷にも見られたように，「包む」ということに独特の美意識を持っています。従って，せっかく持ってきてくれた人の前で，包装を無神経にバリバリと破ることには抵抗があるようです。

　日本に来た外国人がデパートなどで買い物をした時に，丁寧できれいな包装に感心するそうですが，日本人がいかに「包む」ということを大事にするかの表れでもあります。

　しかし，一番の理由は，日本人は他人の前でストレートに喜怒哀楽の感情を表現しない，ということにあります。本当はうれしいのですが，相手の前でうれしい気持ちを表すことに，照れを感じてしまいます。そのためにプレゼントを相手の目の前で開けることができないのです。

Q Why aren't presents opened in front of the giver?

A There are scenes in American movies where a person receives a present, quickly rips off the wrapping and uncovers the present. Even a present nicely wrapped in beautiful Christmas wrapping paper is roughly ripped off. Many Japanese viewing the scene cannot help but feel chagrin at such beautiful paper being roughly treated.

In Japan, there exists a unique sense of the artistic in wrapping paper such as origami, *noshibukuro* (an envelope for a gift of money), and the *furoshiki* (a wrapping cloth), although people using the *furoshiki* have now become fewer in number. The Japanese feel a certain resistance in roughly ripping off the wrapping from a present in front of the giver who took special care in bringing the present especially for the occasion.

People from other countries who shop at department stores in Japan are impressed by how carefully their purchases are wrapped in beautiful paper, an indication of how highly the Japanese regard wrapping to be.

However, the main reason seems to lie with the inability of the Japanese to outwardly show their feelings. Although they are genuinely glad, they are embarrassed to show their feelings in front of others. This makes them unable to open a present in the presence of the giver.

Question なぜ，お金を紙に包んで渡すのですか？

Answer

　買い物の支払いのとき以外に，お金をむき出しで相手に渡すことは失礼だと，今でも多くの日本人は考えています。従って，お金を紙に包んだり，封筒に入れたりして渡すのが普通です。

　葬儀のときの香典，結婚式などお祝いのときに出す祝儀には，日本独特ののし袋というものがありますし，チップを渡すときも，懐紙に包んだり，小さな封筒に入れたりして渡します。

　日本人がこのように金銭に対して，一見，潔癖な姿勢を持っているのは，武士社会の金銭観が大きな影響を持っています。日本の社会を統治してきたのは武士ですが，その武士の生活は，主君から頂戴する扶持で成り立っており，そもそも金儲けという世界とは無縁でした。ですから，金銭欲に対しては否定的な態度をとり，金儲けはよくない行為であり，金銭は不浄なものという考えを，武士は持っていたのです。

　「清貧に甘んじる」という表現もあるぐらいで，金銭欲にとらわれることは恥とも考えてきました。従って，金の話はあからさまにしない，金をむき出しに見せびらかすことはしない，金をむき出しで相手に与えることも失礼，という考えが守られてきたのでしょう。

　そういう金に対する潔癖性が，今の日本人の金に対する感覚にまだ残っているのです。

Q Why is money always wrapped when given?

A Except when purchasing something, many Japanese feel that it is impolite not to have money wrapped when handing it to another person. Money is usually wrapped in paper or placed in an envelope when given to someone.

Monetary funeral offerings and monetary gifts for congratulatory occasions such as weddings are placed in special *noshi* envelopes. Gratuities are wrapped in Japanese tissue or placed in a small envelope before given to the other.

The care given by the Japanese toward money is largely influenced by the warrior society's concept of money. Although it was the samurai who ruled Japanese society, they lived off a stipend received from their master. From the onset, it was a world indifferent to money making. The samurai took a negative stance toward lust for money and considered making money to be undesirable and money itself to be unclean.

There was even an expression *seihin ni amanjiru* meaning to be content to live in honorable poverty. It was considered a disgrace to get caught up with the desire for wealth. Rules concerning money were upheld and still practiced today such as: not speaking bluntly about money, not displaying unwrapped money, and not giving unwrapped money to the other.

The punctiliousness of the Japanese toward money still remains with them to this day.

Question　なぜ，洗濯物を外に干すのですか？

Answer

　ご主人の転勤で，東京のマンションからサンフランシスコの1軒家の生活になった主婦の話ですが，庭が広いのでひもを張って盛大に洗濯物を干したところ，隣の家から苦情が来てびっくりしたそうです。

　アメリカの一般的な家は周囲に塀を巡らせていませんが，だからこそ，その周囲の環境にも価値を求めて家を買っているのだということを，日本人はなかなか理解できません。

　日本では，洗濯物は外に干して，太陽で乾かすのが一番，というのが常識です。従って，天気のいい日の家の庭や，マンションのベランダは洗濯物で満艦飾。だれも文句を言う人はいません。

　第一，狭い日本では住む空間さえ確保できれば上々というわけで，家の中に大型の乾燥機を備えた洗濯室を備える余裕はありません。外に干すより他に手はないのです。しかし最近は，マンションではベランダの柵よりも低い位置に干すなど，少しは周囲の環境を意識するようになってきています。

　また，アメリカではとんでもないこととされている，下着を外に干して人の目にさらすことは，特にマンションの1人暮らしの女性は安全のためにもやめるようになってきましたし，住環境の変化に伴って，日本の洗濯物干しに一工夫をしなければならなくなってきたようです。

Q Why is laundry hung outside to dry?

A A Japanese housewife, upon her move to a house in San Francisco because of her husband's transfer, strung clothes lines in her spacious yard to hang up her big load of laundry to dry. She was bewildered by a complaint made by her neighbor.

There are no fences around a typical American house and there are people who place importance on the surrounding scenery and take it into consideration when buying a house. This is a concept alien to the Japanese.

In Japan, hanging laundry out in the open to dry under the sun has been the norm and looked upon as the best way to dry laundry. On clear days, yards of houses and verandas of condominiums are fully decked out with laundry and with not one complaint made.

In a small country like Japan, having ample living space is the best one could possibly hope for. There is no space for a laundry room equipped with a large dryer. The only recourse is to hang it outside. Recently, a growing awareness of the surrounding environment in Japan has caused the Japanese to hang their laundry in a lower position than the veranda ledge of their condominium.

American might think hanging underwear in the open for all to see is out of the question. Women living alone, for safety, have now abandoned this practice. Along with the change in the living environment, the time has now come for the Japanese to devise other ways of drying their laundry.

Question なぜ，自宅に招待してくれないのですか？

Answer

　日本の平均的な家の大きさは，外国人から見れば実にささやかな規模です。アメリカ映画などで，どんな庶民的な家でも，家の中にゆとりがあるのを見ていますから，それに比べて実に狭い日本の家に人を「招く」となると，少々ためらいが生じます。

　もちろん親しい間柄では，お互いの家に招き合ったりということは，日常よくあります。子供の誕生パーティーに友達を招いたりもします。

　しかし，外国人を招く，しかも1人2人だけではなくて多人数を招いたパーティーとなると，それだけのスペースの居間を持つ家は数少ないのが日本の現状です。ましてガーデン・パーティーができるぐらいの広い庭を持つ家は少ないでしょう。

　仮に環境が整ったにしても，日本では家のウチとソトのことに一線を引くといった考えがあり，仕事仲間を外国のように積極的に家に呼ぶということは少ないかも知れません。

　それに，いざ招くとなったら大仕事と思ってしまい，御馳走はどうしようとかあれこれ迷った挙げ句に，結局やーめた，ということになってしまいます。アメリカではチーズとクラッカー，それにちょっとしたサラダか手料理というメニューで，堂々とパーティーを開くそうで，「もてなし」の基本はやはり「好意」なのだ，ということもわかってはいるのですが――。

Q Why don't the Japanese invite people over to their homes?

A The average size of a Japanese house, as seen by people from other countries, is extremely small. American homes that appear in American movies, no matter how ordinary, all appear to be spacious compared to the cramped conditions of Japanese homes. This makes the Japanese a little hesitant to invite people over.

Of course, among close friends, it is common to invite each other over, and children's friends are invited over for their children's birthday parties.

However, when inviting foreign guests, and not only one or two but many foreign guests to a party, there are very few homes in Japan with a living room large enough to accommodate the guests. There are also very few homes in Japan with yards big enough to hold a garden party.

Even if space poses no problems, the Japanese tend to draw a line between those who are considered insiders and those who are considered outsiders. Unlike in other countries where co-workers are invited over to the home, co-workers are rarely invited over to Japanese homes.

And when an invitation is extended, the Japanese go overboard wondering what to serve the guests and worrying about every little detail. Finally in desperation, they throw up their hands and call it quits. Americans hold parties even though what they can offer is something very simple like cheese, crackers and a salad. Foremost in entertaining is one's good intention, which the Japanese realize all too well, but yet—.

Question　なぜ, 老人に席を譲らないのですか?

Answer

　確かに, 電車・バスなどで, わざわざ席のシートの色を変えて, お年寄りや体の不自由な人が優先的に座る席を作っているのは日本だけだと思います。こんな席を作らなければならないのは, 日本では, 年配の人たちに席を譲らない人が多いからだということになります。

　譲らないのは, 特に, 若い人に目立ちます。これは, 外国の家庭の子供に対するしつけに比べて, 日本の家庭のしつけは非常に甘いことに, 遠い要因があるようです。

　日本では, 子供を連れて電車に乗ってきた母親が, 空いている席に急いで子供を座らせる光景をしばしば目にします。子供も座るのが当然といった顔で駄々をこねます。そんな子に席を譲ってあげる人さえいます。

　寝る時間にしても, 外国の家庭のように厳しくありませんし, 欲しがるものはわりと自由に買い与えています。そんな甘やかされた環境で育ちますから, 大きくなっても, 自分が座るのは当たり前といった無神経さのままなのかもしれません。

　それに, 今の子供たちは, 体格は大きくなっても, 昔に比べて体力が落ち, じっと立っていることができないようです。道端にしゃがみこんでいる無様な姿には, 良識ある日本人は眉をひそめています。

Q Why aren't the elderly offered seats?

A Japan is perhaps the only country were priority seats, which are of a different color from the regular seats, are designated for the elderly and disabled on trains and busses. The need for these priority seats is evidence that there are many Japanese who do not offer their seats to the elderly.

This can particularly be seen in the younger generation. Compared to the strict discipline parents in other countries mete out to their children, children in Japan are overindulged, which may be a remote contributing factor explaining this phenomenon.

One often comes across a mother in Japan get on a train and rush to get her child seated in the first available seat she can manage to find. The child expects to get a seat and becomes unmanageable when the expectation is not met. There are even people who offer their seats to these spoiled brats.

Bedtime is not observed as strictly in Japan as in other countries, and Japanese parents also pamper their children by buying them nearly everything they ask for. Being raised spoiled, these self-centered children grow up feeling they have every right to be seated.

Also, the children of today are not as strong as before although they are built better. They are unable to stand for long periods of time. Japanese with sense frown at the sight of them sunk in a crouch along the roadside.

Question なぜ，たばこをやめられない人がまだ多いのですか？

Answer　　1994年の日本たばこ産業株式会社の調査によると，喫煙者は成人男子の59％，成人女子の14.8％，全体では36.2％だそうです。

　日本で，たばこのケースに「あなたの健康を損ねることがあります。吸い過ぎに注意しましょう」という文句が印刷されるようになったのは，1972年（昭和47年）からです。

　最近では日本でも，飛行機，列車，レストランに禁煙席が増えましたし，オフィス内を禁煙にするという会社も増えました。しかし，アメリカで禁じられているたばこのテレビCMが，日本では堂々と放映されていますし，たばこの生産が国の専売から民営になったのは，まだ11年前のことで，そのたばこの会社が日本ではまだ優良企業の1つであるなど，日本ではたばこはまだ社会的に認知された存在です。

　しかも日本人には，個人に対する攻撃や，責任の追及を避けようとする性向がありますから，たばこの煙がいやだという人も，たばこを吸っている人に面と向かって，吸わないでくれとはなかなか言えません。

　一方，肩身が狭くなったたばこの方は，生き残りのためにタールの量が少ないものを発売して人気を保とうとしています。そのせいか，男子の喫煙者は3年連続で減少しているのに対して，女子の喫煙者は前年よりも1％増えています。

Q Why are there still many Japanese who can't quit smoking?

A According to a 1994 survey by the Japan Tobacco Inc., 59% of adult men and 14.8% of adult women smoked making an overall of 36.2% of adults who smoked.

The warning printed on cigarette packages, "Cigarette smoking is harmful to your health; please refrain from excessive smoking" was issued in Japan in 1972.

Recently, no-smoking sections have increased in airplanes, trains and restaurants in Japan. There is also an increase of companies that prohibit smoking on the office premises. However, unlike in the United States where TV cigarette commercials are banned, cigarette commercials are still openly shown in Japan. It has only been 11 years since tobacco production came under private management from being a state owned monopoly. Tobacco companies are still one of the top-rated companies in Japan, evidence that smoking is still socially accepted.

Because the Japanese try to avoid personal attacks and to hold a person responsible, someone who is bothered by cigarette smoke finds it difficult to confront a smoker to ask him or her to stop smoking.

To survive, the tobacco industry which has been backed into a corner has announced a low-tar brand of cigarette to hold their market share. Perhaps this is what led to a 1% increase of women smokers compared to the previous year as opposed to a three-year consecutive decrease of men smokers.

Question　なぜ，家の中はきれいなのに，公共の場所は汚いのですか？

Answer　少し大げさな言い方になりますが，「都市」とか「公共」ということについて，日本人はあまり意識していないとよく言われます。

欧米の近代都市は整然と開発されたところが比較的多いようですが，日本では，東京にしても大阪にしても，きちんとした都市計画はなく，勝手に人が住み着いて，雑然と発展していったにすぎません。

日本の大都市で，歴史上，計画的に作られたといえば，京都市，北海道の札幌市，戦後の名古屋市ぐらいのものでしょう。

それに，公共の場所の代表である公園の面積は，東京では1人あたり，わずか2㎡だそうです。ワシントンでは1人あたり40㎡前後もあるとか。ワシントンのわずか20分の1しか公共の場がない日本人には，かえって公園や町並みを自分たちの環境の一部として大事にする意識が生まれてこないのだと思われます。

とにかく狭いところに人が集中するわけですから，ごみも多くなるのも当然。それを気にしてもしかたがない，長いものに巻かれろ主義の日本人の性格が，公共の場の不潔さを黙認しているのかもしれません。

Q Why are the inside of homes kept clean but public places kept dirty?

A It may be exaggerating it a little, but it is often said that the Japanese have no concept of "city" or "public."

Modern city development in the West was, on a great part, undertaken in a comparatively systematic fashion, unlike in Japan where there was no proper city planning whether in Tokyo or Osaka. People lived wherever they pleased causing the city to sprawl out haphazardly.

Throughout history, cities in Japan built according to a city plan were few in number. These cities are: Kyoto, Sapporo in Hokkaido, and Nagoya after the war.

A good example of a public area is parks. There are only 2m² (6.3 sq. ft.) of park space per person in Tokyo while it stands more or less at 40m² (129 sq. ft.) per person in Washington D.C. Having only one twentieth of public space than Washington D.C. does not bring about an awareness in the Japanese that parks and cities are a part of one's environment that require care.

Many people are concentrated in a small area and trash is bound to accumulate, but the Japanese feel it is no use attempting to do anything about it. This attitude of, "it's no use fighting city hall" brings about a tacit approval and may be the reason why public places are not kept clean.

Question　なぜ, ラブ・ホテルがこんなに多いのですか?

Answer

　　今はラブ・ホテルとは言わず, レジャー・ホテル, ファッション・ホテル, あるいはブティック・ホテルなどと呼ぶのだそうです。

　　こういうホテルを利用する客は, 恋人たち, 不倫など一時的な恋を楽しむ男女, 一般の夫婦, セックスを商売とする女性とその客となる男たち——など様々です。ある調査によれば, 1日に160万ベッドが利用されているとか!

　　今の日本人は, 恋人同士なら当然, また, 合意の上ならばお互いセックスを楽しむことは自然なことと考えている人も多いですから, 売春・買春行為はともかくとして, ホテルに入ったからといってとがめ立てする理由はありません。

　　そもそも日本には江戸時代に, 待合という, 文字通り, 待ち合わせてデートを楽しむために貸し部屋がありましたし, アメリカだって, 同じ目的のモーテルもあるわけです。

　　問題は, 日本ではすぐにその目的のホテルとわかる外観になっているものが多かったことですが, 最近はぐっと変わって, 普通のホテルと変わらない明るくしゃれたホテルが増えてきています。ラブ・ホテルとは言わず, ファッション・ホテルとも呼ばれるゆえんです。

　　なにしろ, 日本の家は狭いですから, 自宅では自由にセックスを楽しむことは難しく, 必然, 一定の時間で借りられるホテルを利用することになるわけです。

Q Why are there so many love hotels in Japan?

A Formerly called love hotels, these hotels are now called leisure hotels or fashion hotels or boutique hotels.

People utilizing these hotels are lovers, people committing adultery enjoying a moment of passion, husband and wife, women in the sex profession and their male customers, and the list goes on. A survey has it that 1.6 million beds are utilized a day!

The Japanese feel that it is all right to have sex if both partners love each other, and furthermore, many feel that it is perfectly natural to enjoy sex if both partners consent to it. With the exception of prostitution, they feel utilizing these hotels should be no cause for rebuke.

During the Edo period (1600–1868), couples could arrange to meet and enjoy a date in a rented room. In the United States, a motel serves the same purpose.

The exterior of many of these hotels utilized for this purpose in Japan stood out glaringly as being such hotels. There has been a drastic change recently as many of these hotels have sprung up that look no different from other hotels in their spruceness and stylishness, giving reason to call these hotels fashion hotels instead of love hotels.

Houses in Japan are small and it is difficult to freely enjoy sex, hence the necessity to utilize these hotels that can be had for a short period of time.

Question　なぜ，自動販売機でポルノ雑誌やお酒を売っているのですか？

Answer

　日本は様々な規制がある国ですが，一方，一般民衆の権利に気兼ねして，道徳的なことに対しては，個々人が持つ思想，道徳，倫理の尊重ということと，社会生活のための約束ごとの厳守ということを，かなり混同しているところがあるように思われます。

　未成年者は酒を飲んではいけない，未成年者に猥褻なものを見せてはいけないなどと決めたことは，その賛否にいろいろな意見があるとはいえ，一応，現代の日本社会の約束ごととして決めたわけですから，それをきちんと守るための手段を講じなければならないはずです。

　しかし日本では，自動販売機でのお酒の販売は夜11時までと決めてみたり，ポルノもここらへんまではよかろう（このように勝手に決めることがおかしいのですが）という内容のものを，自動販売機で発売することを許可しています。一般の人に不便をかけるから——というのが理由です。

　これは未成年者に対して，酒やポルノは自由に手に入るが，君たちは理性を持って我慢するのだぞ，と言っているだけで，社会的に約束ごとを守らせる手段にはまったくなっていないわけです。個人の自由，言論の自由などと，営業の自由とをはき違えている，と言うことができるでしょう。

Q Why are pornographic literature and alcoholic drinks sold in vending machines?

A Japan is a nation constrained with various regulations, but there is utter confusion on one hand, on a hesitancy on infringing too much on the rights of the general public on moral values such as respecting the thoughts, morals and ethics of each individual; and on the other hand, the necessity of observing strict rules required as members of society.

Although there are pros and cons on views regarding regulations such as prohibiting minors from drinking alcoholic beverages and from viewing obscenity, action should be taken to have these regulations that are laid down by modern Japanese society properly enforced.

However, items that keep within regulations such as sake that is only permitted to be sold until 11 P.M., or pornography that keep within a certain limit (it seems quite strange to set arbitrary rules) are permitted to be sold in vending machines. The reason given is that not selling these items would inconvenience the general public.

This is akin to hanging a juicy carrot before minors and telling them that they should have the good sense to practice self-restraint, which is by no means a way to enforce rules of society. Perhaps individual freedom and freedom of speech have become confused with business freedom.

3

日本人の
好みの
ふしぎ

Puzzling
Tastes of
the Japanese

Question　なぜ，日本人は温泉好きなのですか？

Answer　　日本は梅雨のころから秋の半ばを過ぎるまでは，高温多湿の気候です。じっとり汗ばむ日が続きます。ですから，日本の生活にはどうしても風呂が欠かせず，ヨーロッパの人たちに比べてはるかに風呂好きです。

　その日本人の目の前に，様々な病気にも効能があるという温泉があちこちに湧き出ているのですから，日本人が温泉を愛するのは当然。

　日本は世界の活火山の約10％があるという火山国で，温泉は日本の北から南まで，いたるところに湧き出ています。その数は日本全国で約2万だそうです。

　日本で温泉と認められるのは，温度が摂氏25度以上で，含有成分が所定の割合以上に含まれていることが条件です。

　東京の近くにも熱海，箱根，伊東などの有名な温泉地が控えており，それぞれの温泉地にはたくさんの温泉宿が立ち並んでいます。熱海温泉だけでも，年間に訪れる客は，350万人。日本人にとって，ほっとくつろげる旅は，まずは温泉へ行くことなのです。

　このごろは温泉を好む外国人もふえてきましたから，温泉につかる心地よさは，世界共通のことなのかもしれません。

Q Why are the Japanese fond of *onsen* (hot springs)?

A High temperature and high humidity characterize Japan's climate from June in the rainy season to mid autumn. Unabated sweat drenched days make baths an indispensable necessity in Japan. Compared to Europeans, the Japanese are, by far, fond of taking baths.

Hot springs are located here and there in numerous places and are effective for a variety of illnesses. It is no wonder that the Japanese are fond of hot springs.

Japan is a volcanic country where approximately 10% of the world's active volcanoes are located. About twenty thousand hot springs are located from north to south.

A hot spring qualifies as being a hot spring if the temperature is 25°C (77°F) and above, and if the components stand at or above the prescribed ratio.

There are many well-known hot spring resorts near Tokyo such as Atami, Hakone and Ito and many inns stand side by side along the hot spring resorts. Visitors number 3.5 million per year at Atami onsen alone. A place the Japanese would head for without question to find relaxation and repose is to an onsen.

Many non-Japanese nowadays have developed a fondness for hot springs and a pleasant and relaxing soak in an *onsen* is something that has come to be mutually enjoyed by both Japanese and people throughout the world.

Question　なぜ，やくざは入れ墨が好きなのですか？

Answer

　土器の模様から，日本でも縄文時代に入れ墨が行われていたことが推定されると言われています。古く，古事記，日本書紀にも入れ墨に関する記述があります。

　7世紀以後，室町時代まで，入れ墨に関する文献はありませんが，隠れたところで行われていたようで，近世になると急速に広まっていきます。

　しかし，江戸時代には犯罪者が刑罰として入れ墨を入れられましたので，一般の人がすることは少なくなりました。

　一方，社会のアウトサイダーたちは，自分を誇示するために入れ墨をするようになります。まさに俠客，ヤクザがそうです。そういう連中が入れた入れ墨は，色も鮮やかで，またデザインも多彩で，江戸時代の入れ墨の技術は世界一と言われるようになりました。

　明治時代になった1872年に，政府から禁止令が出ました。しかし，ヤクザや威勢のいい職人たちの間では根強い人気があり，入れ墨を入れる人が途絶えることはありませんでした。

　現代では1つのファッションとして，一部の若い人の間に入れ墨が流行しています。

Q Why do the *yakuza* like to be tattooed?

A From designs on earthenware vessels, it is assumed that tattooing was carried out in Japan during the Jōmon period (ca. 10,000 BC-ca. 300 BC). There are references to tattooing in the *Kojiki* (712 Record of Ancient Matters), Japan's oldest extant chronicle and in the *Nihon Shoki* (720 Chronicles of Japan), the oldest official history of Japan.

From the seventh century until the Muromachi period (1333–1568), no mention was made to tattooing in the various literature, but it was assumed to have been secretly carried out. It spread rapidly in the latter 16th to the 19th centuries.

Because convicts were tattooed as punishment during the Edo period (1600–1868), not many people chose to be tattooed.

As an ostentatious display of themselves, society's outcasts took up tattooing of themselves, as indeed it was with the gangsters and the *yakuza*. Their tattoos were vivid in color and profuse in design. The technique of tattooing in the Edo period was regarded as the best in the world.

The Meiji government in 1872 banned tattooing altogether but it still continued to be immensely popular and continued to have a strong following among the *yakuza* and plucky artisans.

Tattooing has now become a fad among a segment of the younger generation as a way to appear fashionable.

Question なぜ，電車の中で本を読むのが好きなのですか？

Answer

　電車の中で読むのが好きということではなく，本や雑誌を読むのが好きだから，電車の中でも読むのだ，と答えたほうがいいでしょう。

　特に，日本人が気軽に外で本を読むことができる理由として，大人から子供向けまでの様々な週刊誌，そして，ポケットに入る文庫本が普及していることが挙げられるのではないでしょうか。

　特に，人気の漫画週刊誌などは発売日を待ち焦がれて，出るとすぐに買い求めます。そして，道端であろうと電車の中であろうと，みんなむさぼるように読みます。

　文庫はどんな混んだ電車の中でも，ちょっと手を上に上げる余裕さえあれば，周囲に迷惑をかけなくて読むことができますし，値段も安い上に，今やあらゆる分野の優れた出版物が収録されていますので，実に貴重な本の形態です。最近は，最初から文庫版で発売される本も多くなりました。

　加えて大事なことは，日本は治安がいい国で，電車の中も安心。周囲を忘れて本に読みふけっていても，持ち物をひったくられたりすることもありません。家庭や職場，学校にいるより，電車の中の一時がいちばん落ちつく，という人たちさえ多い日本です。

Q Why do the Japanese like to read books on trains?

A The answer should be phrased, they read on trains and elsewhere because they like to read books and magazines, and not because they like to read on trains.

The reason why the Japanese are able to casually read in public is because of the ready availability of various weekly magazines catering to both adults and children alike, and the diffusion of paperback books that can easily fit into a pocket.

Many people eagerly look forward to each new issue of these popular weekly comic magazines. They are snapped up the day they are put on sale and read avidly whether it be by the roadside or on a train.

No matter how congested a train may be, reading a paperback will not inconvenience anyone as long as there is room enough to raise the arms in order to hold the book. Paperback books are inexpensive and contain a variety of genres of quality reading. It is indeed a most useful form of a book. Recently, many of these books are sold from the onset as paperbacks.

It is significant to add that Japan is a safe country even on trains. One can be engrossed in reading and not have any belongings stolen. There are many Japanese who claim they feel more comfortable in the time spent on a train than at home, work or at school.

Question　**なぜ，いい歳をした人たちが漫画を読むのですか？**

Answer　　日本の漫画の世界は，特に，1959年に「少年マガジン」「少年サンデー」などの少年漫画週刊誌が創刊されてから，大きく変わってきました。

　　これらの漫画週刊誌で人気を博したのが，「劇画」と言われるストーリー漫画です。小説に代わって，青少年の心をぐっとつかむ多彩な内容の物語が展開され，現代の英雄ともなっていく漫画の主人公も出てきました。『巨人の星』や『あしたのジョー』などがその代表的な作品です。

　　その後，少年向けだけでなく，少女向けや，そしてその漫画世代が成長するにつれて，青年向け，大人向けの漫画雑誌が次々と誕生していきました。そこにはギャグ漫画から感動的なストーリーまで，様々な内容がありますが，それぞれの年代が鑑賞するに耐えるだけの内容を備えています。

　　このように日本では，漫画も文字，映像と並んで，情報を伝える有力なメディアとして確立しているのですが，海外では，相変わらず子供向けか，一部のマニア向けに限られているため，実体を知らない海外の人の目には，こんなにも多くの大人が漫画を読んでいるのが，奇異にうつるのでしょう。

Q Why aren't people embarrassed to be reading comics at their age?

A The Japanese comic scene underwent great changes particularly in 1959 with the publication of the weekly *shōnen* (boys') comics such as *Shōnen Magazine* and *Shōnen Sunday*.

These weekly comic magazines derived their popularity from the *gekiga* or a long story-type form of comic. Marking a shift from the novel, comics carried various types of stories that completely enthralled their youthful audiences. Heroes and heroines appearing in these comic magazines even became their contemporary heroes and heroines such as *Kyojin no Hoshi* (The Star of the Giant's Team) and *Ashita no Joe* (Joe of Tomorrow).

Girls' comics later appeared after boys' comics and catering to the rising popularity of these comic magazines to a larger audience of various age groups, comic magazines for youths and adults appeared in rapid succession. The contents of these comics varied widely ranging from gag comics to a moving story, but enough is provided in the contents for the enjoyment of all age groups.

Comics in Japan have established itself on par with the written and the visual as an influential form of media to transmit information. Comics in other countries are usually limited to being a form of children's entertainment or being directed to a narrow segment of interest. People overseas who are not familiar with the actual situation might find it strange to see many adults in Japan buried in comics.

**Question　なぜ，時間とお金をかけて，お茶の飲み方を
学ぶのですか？**

Answer　　確かに，たかがお茶の飲み方のノウハウを学
ぶために高い授業料を払うのは，外国人には馬
鹿馬鹿しいと見えるのでしょう。

　しかし，それは単にお茶の飲み方ではなくて，
芸術の域に達しているのが，日本の茶道なので
す。

　これは日本人が小さなことにも完成度を求め
ていく精神に長けていることが，大きな理由で
す。日本語に『求道』という言葉があるように，道
を極めて，精神的にも意味のある世界を作り出
していくのです。

　茶道に用いられるお茶は，日常の生活で飲ん
でいるお茶ではなく，抹茶というものを使いま
すが，その抹茶の入れ方を伝統的に伝え続け，お
茶の入れ方だけでなく，お茶を味わう心をも伝
えようとしているのが茶道です。

　どんな入れ方をするか，どんな器を使うか，ど
んな心構えでお茶を入れるか，また，茶室にどん
な花を飾るか，どんな掛け軸をかけるかまで，気
を遣います。その作法はなかなか奥が深く，学ぶ
には時間と，授業料がかかるわけです。

Q Why are time and money spent on learning how to drink tea?

A People from other countries probably feel it is foolish to pay for costly lessons on something trivial like learning how to drink tea.

However, the Japanese art of tea ceremony is not simply something trivial like drinking tea. *Sadō* (tea ceremony) has attained the level of an art.

This is largely due to the spirit of the Japanese good at seeking perfection in all things no matter how trivial, as expressed in the word *kyūdō*, meaning to thoroughly investigate the way and to create a world with meaning and containing the spiritual.

The tea used in tea ceremony is not ordinary tea drunk everyday, but a special kind of tea called *mattcha* (powdered quality tea). Tea ceremony is an art which has been traditionally handed down through the ages of how to prepare *mattcha*. The art of *sadō* not only shows how to prepare the tea, but also how to have the right frame of mind when savoring the tea.

Care must be taken to follow the right procedures in everything from: the method of preparing the tea, the type of utensils used, one's approach to preparing the tea, the kind of flowers to decorate the tea ceremony room with and the kind of scroll to hang in the room. Mastering these profound rules requires many hours of training and much money.

Question なぜ，電車の中でポルノ新聞や雑誌を読むのですか？

Answer

　日本は保守的，道徳的な国と思われていますが，テレビや雑誌の上での暴力やセックスの記事の規制はアメリカよりゆるやかで，日本の雑誌（特に週刊誌）や新聞（特に夕刊）の中には，外国人の目にはかなりエッチと思える写真や記事が登場しています。

　そんな雑誌や新聞は，そもそもニュースや娯楽記事，小説などを載せており，大衆の貴重な情報源でもあります。そのおまけの部分にちょっとエッチな記事もあって楽しめるように編集されています。

　他に，ポルノと呼ばれる雑誌や本も多数あり，そういうものは公然とは電車の中で読みませんが，やはり，一般の書店の店頭で買うことができます。つまり，性器そのものや，行為そのものを載せなければいいと，出版物におけるエッチの度合いに，都合のいい線を引いているのです。

　ポルノ写真や記事に，ここまではよく，ここまでは悪いという線はないわけですから，成人の見たい人には制限はつけないが，一般の人や子供の目にはつかないように気を遣うというのが海外であることに比べて，日本ではドギツイものはないかわりに，一般の人や子供の目に触れないようにする配慮に欠けるのが問題です。

Q Why are pornographic newspapers and magazines read on trains?

A Japan is considered to be a conservative and a moral country but compared to the United States, Japan is lax on regulations concerning violence and sex on TV and in magazines. Non-Japanese may find pictures and articles appearing in Japanese magazines (especially weeklies) and newspapers (especially the evening edition) to be sexually explicit.

To begin with, these magazines and newspapers are an important source of information containing news reports based on the news of the day or of the week, articles for pure entertainment, and serials of novels, all which are enjoyed by the masses. As a form of added spice, a little risque is thrown into some of the articles and edited to amuse the readers.

There are many other kinds of pornographic books and magazines but they are not read in public on trains although they are readily available in ordinary bookstores. In other words, an arbitrary line is drawn on how far to go as long as the sexual organs and the sexual act itself are not shown.

In other countries, there is no line determining what is considered acceptable and what is considered unacceptable. Although there are no restrictions placed on adults wishing to view such material, care is taken so that the general public and children do not get their hands on such material. In Japan, on the other hand, there are no overly explicit scenes but there is a problem with lax control where the general public and children can have easy access to them.

Question なぜ, ブランドものが好きなのですか?

Answer

　外国から来た人たちが, まずビックリすることの1つは, 若い人たち, 特に女性の外国製品に対するブランド志向だそうです。確かにそうですね。アメリカなどでは, 大学生は自分で働いて学費や生活費をかせぐのが一般的で, とても高いブランドものを買う余裕はないのに, 日本の女子大生の多くが, ブランドもののバッグなどを持っているのですから……

　それも一時はバッグだけとか, 服だけとか, 一点主義だったのが, このところではトータルなファッションにまで波及し, それぞれのブランドで身を固める人たちを, シャネラーとか, グッチャー, ビトナーなどというあだ名で呼ぶようになってきているのだから驚きです。

　階級意識が強いヨーロッパでは, エルメスのケリー・バッグを持っていれば, 上流階級の「お嬢さま」と決まっていて, また他の人もそれを真似しようとは思わないのです。ところが日本は「一億総中流階級」という意識の上, 経済発展によって, 若い人がちょっとアルバイトをしてそれなりのお金を手にいれてしまいますし, また, 親も子供に甘く, つい, 高価なものまで買い与えてしまうことから, ブランド志向が生まれてきたのです。

Q Why are the Japanese so attracted to brand names?

A People coming from abroad are first of all surprised to see the young generation, especially Japanese women, having a weakness for big-name brands. And this is certainly true. It is not unusual for American university students to work to earn their own tuition and living expenses and hence, expensive top-brand articles are out of the reach of many. However, many Japanese university women students own a top-brand handbag or other top-brand goods.

At one time, brands focused on only a single item such as bags or clothes, but nowadays the focus has extended to total fashion. There are some who stick to their respective top-brand articles and are unbelievably called by nicknames such as Chaneller (Chanel), Guccier (Gucci) or Vuittoner (Vuitton).

A young lady carrying a Hermes tote bag in class-conscious Europe indicates that she comes from a good family, but no one particularly shows any interest in imitating her. This infatuation with big-name brands arises from the fact that all Japanese consider themselves as belonging to the middle class that through Japan's economic development makes it possible for the young people to earn extra cash by working at part time jobs as well as the leniency parents show to their children by buying them anything they ask for, even expensive items.

Question　なぜ，日本人はそんなにグルメ好きなのですか？

Answer　　ホームステイでアメリカに行った日本人学生たちが，異口同音に言うのは，アメリカの家庭料理の単調さです。うまいまずいは別にして，ほとんど毎日，冷凍食品を電子レンジでチンしてでき上がりというのですから……

　その点，日本はまだ四季折々の食物が食卓にバラエティ豊かに並べられます。

　また素材だけでなく，和食を中心としながらも，中華料理をはじめとして，フランス料理，イタリア料理などの調理法も家庭に入っていますから，日本人は世界のなかで，もっとも「食」の楽しさを享受している国民なのかもしれません。

　このように舌がこえている上に，なんでも「道」にして究極のものを追求する国民性がありますから，テレビなどでも，料理の「名人」や「鉄人」がもてはやされることになります。

　こういう要素に加えて，経済発展のおかげで，サラリーマン族は「社用族」としての交際費で，また生活に余裕の出てきた主婦たちや若い女性たちは，友達といっしょに，あちらこちらとうまいものを求めて食べ歩くようになり，グルメ・ブームが生まれました。

　今までは料理店と言えば，多くは和食，中華，フランス，イタリアの料理でしたが，スペイン，インド，タイ，ベトナム，ギリシアなどなど，各国の料理店が出てきたのも，グルメ・ブームの結果と言えるでしょう。

Q Why are the Japanese such gourmets?

A Japanese students who have been on homestay visits in the U.S. unanimously cite the monotony of American home cooking. Leaving aside the question of whether it is tasty or not, the standard fare served almost everyday is frozen food warmed up in a microwave oven.

On this point, the Japanese still try to serve a variety of food that changes with the seasons.

Although Japanese-style food is the standard fare served in Japan, not only the ingredients but the art of cooking everything from Chinese, French and Italian food have found a place in the Japanese home, making the Japanese perhaps the world's best connoisseur of food.

While being gourmets, the Japanese have a penchant to develop a concept into an art and to pursue the art to the ultimate. Cooking experts appear on cooking competition programs on TV to test their skills against each other.

Coupled with the above factors, the gourmet boom arose from the high economic growth enabling businessmen to enjoy a high standard of living on company entertainment expense. It has also enabled housewives and young women to have a little extra money on hand to go out with friends to eat at a variety of good eating places.

The gourmet boom has resulted in a number of different ethnic restaurants such as Spanish, Indian, Thai, Vietnamese, Grecian in addition to the already existing Japanese, Chinese, French and Italian restaurants.

Question なぜ，こんなにカタカナの言葉を使いたがる
のですか？

Answer　　これは，古く明治時代から西欧化の政策が取
られ続けた結果でもあります。特に，太平洋戦争
の後，日本に英語と欧米文化がどっと流れこん
できますが，その意味やニュアンスを受け止め
ることは，日本語の語彙の範囲では難しく，その
ままカタカナで取り入れられるものが多くなり
ました。

　　明治時代には，英語の概念を何とか日本語に
しようと努力したことがあります。scienceを「科
学」，liberty を「自由」とするなど，新しい日本語
が作られています。しかし，漢字自体の使用が制
限されている現代では，あっさりとカタカナの
まま取り入れられていくようになりました。

　　ちなみに，漢字のみの中国では，当然のことな
がら，すべてを漢字に置き換える作業をしてい
ます。たとえばクリントン大統領は「克林頓」と
するということを，国営通信社である新華社が
決め，全国でそれを統一しています。

　　日本でもカタカナ語を使うことに異論を唱え
る人は多いのですが，日本語自体が中国語や韓
国語から入ってきた語から成り立っていますか
ら，言葉の借用ということについては，日本は寛
大なのだと思います。

Q Why do the Japanese like to adopt foreign words into their language?

A The policy of Westernization undertaken from the Meiji period (1868–1912) is exerting its influence even today. The defeat at the end of World War II caused Western culture and English to flow into Japan. Because of the difficulty in expressing English meanings and nuances within the limits of the Japanese vocabulary, many of these English words were used as they were and adopted in *katakana* form (a noncursive form of writing typically used to write loanwords).

During the Meiji period, efforts were made to express in some way, English concepts into Japanese. Many new Japanese words came into being such as *kagaku* (science) and *jiyū* (liberty). However, with the limitations placed on the use of Kanji today, English words are simply adopted and used as they are.

In a country like China, everything is, of course, written in characters. President Clinton's name is written as 克林頓. The New China News Agency selects and standardizes the characters to be used throughout China.

Many Japanese object to the use of loan words, but the Japanese used today is derived from many words borrowed from Chinese and Korean, evidence that Japan is tolerant to words borrowed from other languages.

Question　なぜ，桜の花がそんなに好きなのですか？

Answer

「桜の樹の下には屍体が埋まっている！」という，梶井基次郎という日本の小説家の名言がありますが，日本人は桜に対して，一般の花とは違った特別の「思い入れ」を持っているようです。

桜は，長い冬が明けて，だいたい1週間から10日の間に，一気に咲き，一気に散っていきますから，武士道に生きたサムライのいさぎよさが，桜の花にたとえられ，「敷島の大和心を人問わば，朝日ににおう山桜花」と短歌に歌われてもいました。

それに，桜ほど本数が多く，かつ北から南まで広く日本全国に分布していて，しかも，こんなに華やかに花を咲かせる木は他にありません。

桜に先立って梅や桃の木も日本全国に花を咲かせますが，梅の花が咲くころは，春といっても初春で，まだ寒い日が続いています。桃の花はもう少し暖かくなって咲きますが，木の数は桜に比べて多くありません。桜は陽気がよくなってから咲きますから，大きく枝を張って盛大に咲く花の下に，人々を呼び寄せていくのです。

花見という習慣は，昔，貴族階級には欠かせない行事でした。それが庶民の間に広がったものですが，暗い冬の気候が続いた後，ぱっと明るく咲いた桜の下でする花見は，日本人には欠かせないものになっています。

Q Why is the cherry blossom (sakura) cherished?

A There is a well-known saying by the Japanese novelist, Kajii Motojiro (1901–32), "A dead body lies under the sakura tree" referring to the contrast between the beautiful and the eerie. The Japanese feel a special intensity particularly for the sakura.

After the end of a long winter, within a period of a week to ten days the sakura bursts into bloom and falls all at once; hence, they are compared to the manliness of a samurai abiding by bushido, or the samurai code of behavior. The sakura is also mentioned in the tanka verse, "The spirit of the Japanese can be likened to that of the wild sakura viewed in the morning sun".

There is no other tree as many in number as the sakura that ranges extensively from north to south throughout Japan and that blooms so spectacularly.

Both the plum and peach trees bloom throughout Japan even before the sakura, but the plum blooms in early spring when it is still cold. The peach blooms when it becomes a little warmer, but there are not as many peach trees as there are sakura trees. The sakura blooms when the weather is pleasant and summons the people under its large canopy laden with blossoms.

The custom of viewing the sakura was from old, an event enjoyed by the nobility that later spread to the common people. Sakura viewing under the brilliant and luxuriant blossoms after a long and dark winter has now become a not-to-be-missed event.

4

日本人の
性格の
ふしぎ

The Puzzling
Character of
the Japanese

Question なぜ，日本人はノーとはっきり言えないのですか？

Answer

確かに日本人は，相手からの頼みに対して，本当は断るつもりなのに，その場できっぱりと断れずに，よく「わかりました。考えておきます」「検討します」などと答えます。

これが日本人同士なら，相手の表情や言い方で，どの程度本気で検討するのか，あるいはダメなのかがわかるのですが——。日本は，そんな察し合うことができる文化を持っています。

しかし，外国の人にわかりにくいのは当然でしょう。まして，通訳を通して聞いたのでは，文字通りに受け取ってもしかたがありません。

相手は，もしかしたら——と思って期待をしたあげく，結局は断られることになりますが，この場合，単に断られたというよりも，裏切られた気持ちにさせてしまうことが問題ですね。

これは，常に相手の立場を考えて和を保とうする日本人の控え目さを表しているようですが，日本人の優柔不断の現れとも言えます。

そういう日本人の性質にも原因がありますが，同時に，日本の会社の意思決定のシステムにも原因があります。日本では，通例，意思決定は広く幹部の合議に基づくことが多く，仮にトップであれ独断専行はできないようです。小規模のワンマン会社であれば，意思決定はかなり早いはずです。

Q Why can't the Japanese say no?

A When the Japanese want to turn down a favor asked of them, they feel that a flat refusal would hurt the feeling of the other, so they end up saying, "I see, I'll think about it," or "I'll consider it."

By facial expression and how it is expressed in words the Japanese know to what extent the request will be considered or turned down by the other . Japan's culture is one that enables a person to perceive the intent of the other.

Who can blame the poor foreigner for not knowing what is meant and much more so by hearing it through an interpreter which leaves no room for doubt but to take it literally.

The problem that arises is that the other person has the expectation that perhaps the request would be granted only to find out in the end that it was met with refusal. They then feel deceived rather than refused.

This stems from the discretion perpetually shown to the other person's standpoint to maintain harmony, as well as indecisiveness on the part of the Japanese.

The disposition of the Japanese also plays a role as well as the decision-making system of Japanese companies. Decision making in Japan is, as a rule, largely based on consultation among the management. Even top management is not able to act on its own authority. However, decision making is carried out speedily in a small-scale dictatorially run company.

Question　なぜ，日本人の挨拶は大げさなのですか?

Answer

　　日本の挨拶の基本はおじぎです。最近は握手もごく普通の挨拶になってきましたが，握手は近代になって欧米から入ってきたもので，今でもなじまない日本人がたくさんいます。

　　握手でお互いの手をにぎるぐらいならいいけれど，キスや抱擁のように顔を接触させる挨拶となると，自然にできる日本人はごくごく少ないでしょう。

　　握手という挨拶のしかたは，大きな体の動きはありませんし，そばで見ていてもお互いが対等な印象を受けます。それに比べておじぎには，両者の上下の関係が現れるようです。

　　日本でも仲間の間の挨拶は，「やあ」と軽く手を上げたり，「じゃ」と軽く頭を下げる程度で，決して大げさではありません。しかし，どちらかが目上のときは，どうしても目下の方の人が相手より深く頭を下げるようになります。

　　一般に，年配の婦人のおじぎは実にていねいです。中には握手をしながら，深くおじきまでしてしまう人がたくさんいます。しかも何度も何度もおじぎをする人もいます。

　　この深く，しかも2度,3度と繰り返すおじぎが，外国の人にとって大げさに見えるのではないでしょうか。

Q Why do the Japanese exaggerate their greetings?

A The basic form of greeting in Japan is the bow.
Although shaking hands has now also become accepted
as a form of greeting, the handshake was introduced into
Japan from the West rather recently, so there are many
Japanese today who are still not used to shaking hands.

The Japanese can easily manage the handshake if it can
be carried out simply by grasping the hand of the other, but
there are few Japanese who can spontaneously greet each
other with facial contact such as by kissing or hugging.

The handshake does not require any great body move-
ments and the handshake gives an impression that both parties are of equal standing, while in the bow there is a distinct
superior-inferior relationship.

However, greetings between friends are fairly informal
and are not exaggerated at all. For example, they would
casually raise their hands with a simple "Ya!" (Hi!), or lightly lower their heads with a "Ja!" (Bye!). However, when
one party's position is higher than the other, the person in
the lower position bows his or her head a little lower than
the person in the higher position.

Generally speaking, older women bow very politely.
There are many who bow deeply while shaking hands at the
same time, and there are others who bow many, many
times.

Bowing deeply and repeating it a number of times may
strike non-Japanese as going a little too far.

Question なぜ，すぐに個人的なことを尋ねるのですか？

Answer

　よく指摘されることですが，日本人は道であったときの挨拶として，「どちらにお出かけですか」と聞きます。答えは「ちょっとそこまで」とか，「ちょっと買い物に」とか，当たり障りのない返事になりますが，確かに，どこに行こうと相手の勝手で，何も詮索するような挨拶である必要はないわけです。また「ご結婚は？」とか，「お子さんは？」とか，プライバシーに立ち入ったことも，つい，聞いてしまいます。

　この理由として，農耕社会の家族主義的な付き合いの中や，また封建的な家制度に縛られていた中で，日本人が個人の自由というものから比較的に縁遠かったことが挙げられます。

　相手の境遇を知ることがプライバシーに踏み込む，という意識はありません。むしろ相手に対する仲間意識の現れで，相手と交際できるかどうかを察し合っていると言えます。

　農村部ではもちろん，都会の下町のほうでも，親しく出入りする交際があり，「下町人情」として，このほうがいいと言う人もいました。

　しかし，都会に人が集中し，アパートで隣の人とも没交渉で過ごす人も多くなった現代では，日本でもプライバシーを大事にする人たちが増え，最近では，あまり立ち入って挨拶はしなくなってきました。

Q Why are the Japanese quick to ask personal questions?

A As is often pointed out, a typical greeting in Japan when meeting someone on the street is, "Where are you going?" And the answer would be a noncommittal, "Just over there," or "Just shopping." It is not anyone's business where the other is going, so there is no need for the greeting to be taken at face value. Also, the Japanese have no scruples about asking personal questions such as, "When are you getting married?" or "No children yet?"

The reason stems from Japan's agrarian society where everyone was considered family, as well as constraints imposed by a feudalistic family structure where individual freedom was relatively unheard of.

No one considered personal information about a person to be an intrusion on his or her privacy. It was seen as camaraderie, of feeling each other out to see if the other could be included in one's circle of acquaintances.

This was true in the farming villages and even in cities in the *shitamachi* area, or the traditional working class neighborhoods. The *shitamachi* neighbors were on very friendly terms with one another. There are some who prefer this camaraderie of the warmheartedness of *shitamachi*.

However, people who respect privacy have increased with the huge concentration of people living in cities and the large number of people who have no contact at all with their neighbors in their apartment buildings. There is a tendency nowadays not to ask prying questions.

Question　なぜ，日本人はこんな高物価に黙っていられるのですか？

Answer　　経済企画庁では，毎年，物価を欧米の4都市と比較した数字を発表していますが，それによれば，1993年の東京の物価は，ニューヨークの1.41倍，ロンドンの1.46倍，パリの1.3倍，ベルリンの1.38倍だったとのことです。

　確かに，外国から来た人は，日本の物価の高さに驚きます。特に1990年代に入ってからは円高の影響をまともに受けて，外国の人たちが深刻にならざるをえないことはわかります。

　しかし，物価というのはそれぞれの国の経済構造で決まってくるもので，日本は日本なりに，この50年の経済成長で国民所得が上がり，その経済力を背景とした物価です。

　ですから，実感としては物価は安くないと思いながらも，日本人の国民所得から見れば，生活ができなくなる高さではないので，それなりに納得というか，やむをえないことと思っています。つまり，物価が高いかどうかより，安定しているかどうかに関心を持っているのです。

　1990年に入って低成長の時代に入り，国民所得の伸びは止まりましたが，一方，価格破壊などによって，物価も調整されており，日本人が物価を深刻に考えるまでには至っていませんが，このまま所得が伸びず，物価が上がってくることになれば，日本人だって黙っていません。

Q Why don't the Japanese complain about the high prices?

A According to the Economic Planning Agency's annual report comparing prices in four Western cities, Tokyo's prices were 1.41 times higher than New York, 1.46 times higher than London, 1.3 times higher than Paris, and 1.38 times higher than Berlin.

Visitors from other countries are amazed at Japan's high prices. The high appreciation of the yen, particularly in early 1990 is an impact the Japanese realize all too well the visitors are forced to contend with.

Prices are determined by the structure of each country's economy, and Japan's economy is based on its economic strength stemming from the rise in its national income of fifty years of economic growth.

The Japanese realize that prices are not low, but based on their national income, they feel that prices are not so high that they are unable to afford what they need to live on. They either accept it or feel it is unavoidable. They are more concerned about prices being stable than too high.

The early 1990s ushered in a period of low economic growth which saw a cessation in the rise in the national income. Although prices were adjusted through price cutting, the Japanese still have not come to the point of giving serious thought to prices. But even the Japanese will not keep quiet if income failed to keep up with price increases.

Question　なぜ，酔っぱらいにあんなに我慢していられるのですか？

Answer　　日本人が酔っぱらいに寛大であることは否定できないかもしれません。

　　家族主義的な雰囲気の日本の会社の人間関係を保つためには，どうしても付き合いというものが欠かせません。誘われたらむげには断れないのです。そこで，同僚とちょっと一杯ということにもなります。同時に，気の合った友だちと飲むのも楽しいものです。

　　となりますと，お酒の度を過ごす人が出てきます。特に迷惑なのは電車の中の酔っぱらいです。しかし，だれでもが我が身にそれなりのやましさを経験していますから，見て見ぬふりをしてしまいます。

　　というのも，日本人は西欧人に比べて，体質的に酒に弱いということがあるからです。酔った状態を作るのはアルコールがアルデヒドになって神経や血管に影響を与えるからですが，アルコールをアルデヒドに変えるアルコール脱水素酵素が，日本人の80％は異型で，早くアルデヒドを作るのだそうです。

　　さらに，アルデヒドを無害なものにするアルデヒド脱水素酵素は，日本人の50％が作用の遅い2型なのだそうです。白人，黒人は，必ず，早く作用する1型です。つまり，日本人は酔い回りが早く，酔いがさめるのが遅いわけです。

Q Why are drunks tolerated?

A It cannot be denied that the Japanese are tolerant toward drunks.

In a family-structured type of society like Japan, associating with others is essential to maintain good human relationships. It is difficult to turn down an invitation of one's own volition and many Japanese end up going drinking with one's co-workers, but at the same time, drinking with like-minded friends is a pleasure.

There are some who have had a little too much to drink and make a nuisance of themselves, especially on trains. People pretend not to see them for they feel that they are not in a position to pass judgment when they themselves have done something to be ashamed of.

Compared to Westerners, the Japanese have a predisposition to a lower tolerance to alcohol. A state of drunkenness arises when alcohol converts to aldehyde and affects the nerves and blood vessels. Alcohol dehydrogenase, which converts alcohol to aldehyde, is atypical in 80% of the Japanese in that aldehyde is produced too quickly.

Furthermore, 50% of the Japanese belong to the slow-reacting type II form of aldehyde dehydrogenase, an enzyme that makes aldehyde harmless. Whites and blacks belong to the fast-reacting type I form of aldehyde. In other words, the Japanese get drunk faster and stay drunk longer.

Question　なぜ，母親はあんなに子供に甘いのですか？

Answer

　昔，武士の社会では厳しいしつけが行われていました。家庭内は言うにおよばず，家の外でも人にきちんと応対ができなければ，一人前の人間として認められませんでした。従って，家庭内で母親も厳しいしつけの役を果たしていました。

　しかし，明治になって武士の世界もなくなり，日本人に西欧の自由主義的な考えが流入してきましたし，太平洋戦争後は家制度が廃止され，家庭は夫婦とその子供を核として構成されるようになりますから，家制度などを通して社会につながっていたしつけの規範といったものはなくなってしまいました。

　特に敗戦によって，それまで権威を持っていたいろいろな価値観が大きく壊れた結果，大人あるいは父親の権威が失墜し，子供を叱ることができなくなったようです。従って，親子が和気あいあいと過ごす現代家庭が誕生するのですが，外を見れば，激しい進学競争，就職戦線。企業戦士の父親は仕事の帰りは遅いし，子供の教育は母親任せ。

　母親には，やはり可愛い我が子。可愛がることと，甘やかすことが混同してしまっていますし，さらに問題であるのは，親が子供を自分の付属物にしてしまっていることかもしれません。

Q Why are Japanese mothers overly soft on their children?

A Warrior society of long ago maintained strict discipline. One was not recognized as a full-fledged adult unless one could properly deal with people one came across outside of the home, to say nothing of within the home. The mother also took on the role of a strict disciplinarian at home.

Warrior society came to an end in the Meiji period (1868–1912) and liberalism, which was introduced from the West, made its way into Japan. The end of World War II saw the demise of the family institution which gave rise to the nuclear family comprised of a husband and wife and their children. This led to priority not being placed in observing these disciplinary precepts that were cultivated within the family institution and which were values required as members of society.

The defeat in the war caused authoritarian values to crumble resulting in adults losing power and making fathers unable to reprimand their children. The modern family evolved where the children grow up in a comfortable family atmosphere. But the world outside of the family is one of extreme competition to get into good schools and to get good jobs. With the corporate warrior father coming home late from work, the responsibility for educating the children falls entirely on the mother.

The mother sometimes brings up the children with too much love. The line between loving a child and spoiling a child becomes blurred. A problem is that some parents regard their children as being their exclusive property.

Question なぜ，選挙の連呼にあんなに我慢していられるのですか？

Answer

　　日本の選挙の連呼は，一種のコマーシャル・ソングみたいなものでしょうが，どちらかと言えば日本人もへきえきしています。「やめてくれーっ」と思っている人が大半です。だいたい，連呼で票が集まるなんて考えられません。

　　日本の選挙では，人に見えないところで買収などの不正が行われるからという理由で，戸別訪問が禁止されています。その代わりというと変ですが，各地域を回って，どの家にも名前が聞こえるように叫び立てることは許されているのです。

　　戸別訪問を認めると不正が行われると心配すること自体が，日本の民主主義のレベルの低さを表していますが，さて，法律で認められたこの制度をやめさせるには，厄介な手続きが必要です。

　　まず，住民運動で署名を集め，議員に働きかけ，法律の改正の案を作らせ，それを議会にかけて——ああ，いつ実現するでしょう！

　　日本は議会民主主義制ですから，議員が言い出してくれればすぐに変わりますが，議員は自分が当選してきた制度を積極的に変えようとは思ってくれません。

　　総理大臣は国民のあずかりしらないところで誕生していくし，政治が遠いものになっている日本では，連呼制の廃止などむなしい運動に終わると，賢い日本人はあきらめているのです。

Q Why do the Japanese put up with all the noise at election time?

A The repeated calls made for a particular candidate during election time is akin to a repeated commercial broadcast that even the Japanese find too much to take. Most of them feel like crying out, "Stop it!" It is preposterous to even think that votes can be garnered by these repeated calls.

Door-to-door soliciting of votes is prohibited in Japan because of the possibility of illegal vote buying through backdoor means. Although it sounds absurd, as an alternative, it is legal to go to different areas with a loudspeaker to drum up loud support for a particular candidate to be heard by everyone living in the area.

The concern that legalizing door-to-door solicitation will result in cheating reflects the low level of Japan's brand of democracy. And outlawing what is already legal requires going through a lot of red tape.

Signatures must first of all be collected through a citizen's movement. A member of the Diet must then be pressured to write a proposal to revise the law, and it must then be brought before the Diet. The question is when.

Japan's government is based on parliamentary democracy. Change will come about quickly if it is proposed by a member of the Diet, but members of the Diet do not actively seek change from the very system that elected them to office.

The prime minister is chosen behind closed doors and politics have become a distant entity to the Japanese. Smart Japanese have resigned themselves to the fact that attempting to abolish campaign noise will only be in vain.

Question　なぜ，日本人は外国人の日本観を知りたがるのですか？

Answer

　　日本人は自己を主張するよりも，集団の和を重んじる国民性を持っており，その集団の中で，自己の評価は他人（世間）の評価によって支えられているかを，しきりと意識していると，よく言われます。

　　その評価が下がるときに「恥をかく」ことになるのですが，その「恥をかく」ことを極端に恐れます。特に，昔の武士は「恥をかくよりも死んだほうがまし」と思ったぐらいです。

　　そこで，人が自分のことをどう思っているかが気になり，なんとかして相手の考えを聞き出すことによって，恥をかく前に対策を講じようとしてしまうのです。

　　日本は江戸時代（1600—1868）の長い間，鎖国政策をしていました。ですから，外国がどのように日本を見ていようと，我関せずに生きてくることができました。

　　しかし，明治以降，西洋の思想，文明がどっと流れこんできましたし，また，太平洋戦争の敗戦という苦い経験も重ねて，その後，駆け足で世界の民主主義国家の仲間入りをしなければならなくなりました。

　　ですから，世界の仲間入りをして恥をかかないように，世界の中の自分たちの姿を外国の人がどう見ているのかを，日本人は常に，どうしても外国人の日本観を通して知りたくなるわけです。

Q Why are the Japanese so interested in hearing about what non-Japanese think about Japan?

A A trait of the Japanese is to place importance on harmony within the group rather than on self-assertion. It is often said that the Japanese are constantly tuned in to what the other thinks to determine their own standing by the appraisal of the other.

One feels feels shame when the appraisal drops and shame is something feared to the extreme. The warriors of long ago preferred dying to being put to shame.

Because the Japanese are so concerned about how they appear to the other, they devise measures beforehand to try to pry information out of the other to avoid being put to shame.

The Japanese were not concerned about how people viewed their country during its long period of isolation under the closed-door policy during the Edo period (1600–1868).

However, Western thoughts and culture inundated Japan during and after the Meiji period (1868–1912), and its crushing defeat in World War II caused Japan to attempt to hurriedly catch up in an effort to join the ranks of the democratized nations.

Now that Japan has joined their ranks, there is a curiosity to find out how Japan appears through the eyes of people in other countries in order not to be put to shame.

Question　**なぜ，日本人は正直で，拾ったものをちゃんと届けるのですか？**

Answer　確かに外国で財布を落とせば，まず絶対に出てこないと言われるのに比べて，日本ではかなりの確率で落とし物が出てきます。しかしこの理由は，日本人が正直だからということでもなさそうです。

　落とし物に関して言えば，日本人は子供のころから「落とし物を拾ったら，必ず交番に届けなさい」と言われてきました。ですから，今でも10円を拾って，交番に届ける正直な子供が日本にいます。

　その「交番」という日本の警察組織の末端が，落とし物の発見に大きな役割を果たしていると断言できます。

　日本の交番の数は，1995年現在，全国に6498箇所あります。これほど地域の隅々に警察の目が行き届いている国はありません。日本は「警察国家」だと悪口を言われることもあるほどです。

　落とし物をした場合でも，近くの交番にすぐに届ければ，比較的早く，見つけだすこともできます。

　仮に出来心で落とし物をネコババしても，優れた日本の警察の捜査力をもってすれば，案外あっさり御用となることを考えると，日本では落とし物は，決して自分では拾わないか，拾ったら正直に交番に届けるのが無難です。

Q Why are the Japanese so honest in returning lost articles?

A It is said that in other countries, an owner never gets back his or her lost wallet, while in Japan the chances are high that the wallet will be returned to its rightful owner, but not because the Japanese are honest.

The Japanese have been told since little that lost articles must always be turned in to the *kōban* (police box). There are honest children in Japan who find 10 yen (10 cents) and dutifully turn it in to the *kōban*.

The *kōban*, at the end of the police organization, effectively fulfills a role in finding lost articles.

As of 1995, 6,498 *kōban* were located throughout Japan. There is no other country where the police keep a sharp eye out in every corner of the country as Japan. Japan is sometimes criticized as being a police state.

When an article is lost, the best way to get it back quickly is to report it to the nearest *kōban* without delay.

If on a sudden impulse, someone decides to keep the lost article, the superb investigative ability of the Japanese police will see to it that the person is arrested, something which the Japanese know all too well. When a lost article is spotted, it is either not picked up or if it is picked up, it is brought to the *kōban* just to be on the safe side.

Question　なぜ，日本人はこんなによく働くのですか？

Answer

　　1993年の年間総実労働時間は，アメリカでは1976時間，それに対して日本では1966時間だそうです。この数字を1970年と比較してみると，350時間以上も減っています。これは貿易黒字が巨大になり，海外から批判されたことや，経済的にゆとりのできた日本人自身が，今度は時間的なゆとりを要求し始めたのが原因です。

　　ですから，数字の上では，もはや「エコノミック・アニマル」とか「ワーカホリック」と呼ばれた高度成長期の日本人に対する表現はあたりません。

　　しかし，実際には長距離通勤や，会社の接待，あるいは残業時間として申告しないサービス残業など，実際に会社に拘束されている時間は，アメリカ人を上回っていると思われます。

　　日本で有給休暇を取らない人の32.7%が，最も多い理由として「休んでいる間，同僚に迷惑をかけるから」を挙げています。

　　若い人の間では，仕事と自分をきっちり分けていく考えに徹した人も多くなり，昔に比べて自由に転職をしていきますし，最初から正式の雇用とは違った契約を求める人もいます。しかし，まだ，多くの日本人に，会社は自分との運命共同体という意識がありますから，実際の数字以上の貢献を会社にしているのが実情なのです。

Q Why do the Japanese work so hard?

A In 1993, the total number of actual working hours in the United States was 1,976 hours while it was 1,966 hours in Japan. This was a decrease of more than 350 hours compared to the figure in 1970. This was due to criticism from abroad concerning Japan's huge trade surplus coupled with the desire on the part of the Japanese, having become comfortable economically, wishing to have more free time for themselves.

Expressions once used to describe the Japanese as "economic animals" and "workaholics" during the period of high economic growth no longer apply.

However, the long commute to and from work; entertaining company guests; and "service overtime," in other words, working overtime without pay are not recorded. The hours a Japanese businessman is actually bound to the company probably exceeds that of the American businessman.

The reason frequently given in 32.7% of the cases for not taking their well-deserved paid vacation was, "will cause inconvenience to colleagues when gone."

There are many in the younger generation who staunchly draw a line between work and themselves. Compared to workers of before, they have no qualms about changing jobs and there are even some who, from the onset, seek a contract which differs from a regular one. However, a great many Japanese feel that it is their destiny to be bound to their company for better or for worse. They spend more hours at the company than what the figures indicate.

Question　なぜ, 他の人がやっていることと同じことをしたがるのですか?

Answer

　日本人は「和」を尊ぶ国民だと外国人に言われます。これは言葉を換えれば, 集団でなければ行動できない国民だとも言えます。確かに, ツアーを組んで, ニューヨークやパリの町を歩き回る日本人の観光団体などの姿が, 世界の人たちの目に焼きついているようです。

　確かにこの集団主義は日本人の特性であり, 「和」に対して, 最も高い優先順位を置きます。「和をもって貴しとなす」という言葉は早くも604年に, 聖徳太子によって作られた憲法十七条の中の第1条として出てくるほどです。

　日本は島国であり, 狭い国土の中のわずかな耕作地に, 多くの人間がしがみついていた農耕社会でした。水を共同で使わなければならない農耕社会では, 多くの場合「村」が形成され, 個々の農作業も村の共同体の中でこそ成り立っていたのです。村の中の「和」を乱せば, 村八分になってしまいます。

　基本的に共同利益を追求する集団の中にいれば, 利益の配分を受け, 保護を与えてもらえるわけです。集団でいることの安心を知っているのが日本人です。

　流行にしてもそうで, 周囲の人がやっていることをやっていれば, 決して自分だけが恥をかくこともないのです。

Q Why do the Japanese want to take up what the others are doing?

A People from other countries refer to the Japanese as a people who revere harmony. In other words, the Japanese cannot act unless they are in a group. The sight of Japanese tourists descending in droves on New York, Paris, etc. on sightseeing tours must no doubt leave a lasting impression on people throughout the world witnessing this spectacle.

Group conformity is a characteristic of the Japanese and harmony is accorded the highest priority. As early as 604, Prince Shotoku wrote, "Harmony is to be accorded the highest reverence." This was even included in the first article in the Seventeen Article Constitution instituted by Prince Shotoku.

Japan is an island country based on an agrarian society where many people made a living clinging to the little arable land available in a small country. Water had to be shared and in many cases, a village was formed and the villagers pitched in helping each other with agricultural work. A person was ostracized by the village for not maintaining harmony.

Basically, if one is a member of the group seeking communal benefits, one would receive a part of the distributed benefits as well as protection from the group. The Japanese know all too well the security offered by the group.

Fads work the same way. One will not have to suffer humiliation alone if one does what the others are doing.

Question なぜ，日本人は血液型で人の性格を決めたがるのですか？

Answer

　日本人のだれもが血液型で性格を判断できると考えているわけではありません。しかし，程度の差はあれ，相当の人が気にしています。日本に来たら血液型をよく聞かれるので，初めて自分の血液型をチェックしたという外国人も多いはずです。

　日本人が血液型占いに弱いのは，日本の家が家父長制度に守られてきて，その家に引き継がれる「血」を重んじてきたからです。明治時代以降の国家主義の影響で，日本人を民族的に純粋だと錯覚してきたことも，「血」を重んじることに拍車をかけてきたのでしょう。

　ですから，1916年に発表された，血液型と性格を結び付ける学説が，日本でブームになったことはうなずけます。血液型の発見自体が19世紀後半のことで，近代の科学主義に支えられて，説得性がある説だったのです。

　日本ではその後，1930年代，そして，1970年から1980年代にかけてブームを起こしています。1970〜1980年にかけては，様々な占いのブームも背景になっています。

　A型の人は神経質，B型の人は大ざっぱ，O型の人の包容力があり，AB型の人はクール——といった性格の分け方をするのが普通ですが，さて，あなたの血液型は？

Q Why do the Japanese want to group person-alities according to blood types?

A Not all Japanese think that blood type has a bearing on personality. However, to some extent, a great number of people show some interest. There are probably many non-Japanese who, upon setting foot in Japan, are asked their blood type and go to have their blood type checked for the very first time.

The reason why the Japanese fall for fortune telling by blood type is because Japan has traditionally maintained a patriarchal family system that places importance on blood-line that will be inherited by the family. From the Meiji period (1868–1912) onward, nationalistic influences subjected the Japanese to be under the illusion that they were a racially homogeneous group of people, which further promoted the importance placed on blood.

It is understandable why the theory linking personalities to blood types that was formulated in 1916 was such a big hit in Japan. Blood type was discovered in the late nineteenth century and the theory, based on modern scientific principles, was very convincing.

The fad was later generated in the 1930s and also from the 1970s to the 1980s. There were many other types of fortune telling fads already in existence in the 1970s to the 1980s.

Generally, A-type people are said to be nervous, B-type people careless, O-type people tolerant, and the AB type cool. What is your blood type?

Question　なぜ，家計を妻に任せるのですか？

Answer　総理府の調査によると，家計費を管理してい
るのは，夫5.2%，妻79.4%，両者11.8%となってい
ます。一方，アメリカは夫14.6%，妻36.5%，両者
45.5%だそうです。日本では圧倒的に主婦が家計
を管理しています。

　日本の家は家父長制度で保たれていましたか
ら，亭主関白に思えますが，実は昔から，家のこ
とは妻に任せるという慣習が強かったようで
す。その慣習が現代でも残っているわけです。
　江戸時代の武家や大きな商家では，妻は家長
の命令に従いますが，奥向きのこと（家計）の責
任は妻が負っていることが多かったのです。明
治以降も，中流以上の家では，この関係が保たれ
ていました。欧米では財布のひもを夫が握って
いるそうですが，日本では男が家計の細かいこ
とに口を出すのは，恥とも思われていました。

　一般庶民の場合は夫婦関係には上下があまり
なく，夫婦で一緒に働き，妻はその上に家事・育
児も担当したわけです。その家が亭主関白にな
るか，かかあ天下になるかはその夫婦の力関係
次第ですが，基本的には日常の支出や貯金のや
りくりは，やはり妻が財布のひもを握っていた
ようです。

Q Why is managing the family budget left entirely to the wife?

A According to a survey by the Prime Minister's Office, the breakdown of those managing the family budget in Japan is as follows: husband 5.2%, wife 79.4%, and both 11.8%. In the United States, the breakdown is as follows: husband 14.6%, wife 36.5%, and both 45.5%. There are more wives managing the family budget in Japan.

Japan has long maintained a patriarchal family system where the husband appeared to control everything, but actually, the custom of the wife managing the affairs of the family was pervasive. This custom has survived to the present day.

The wife obeyed the orders of the family head in the samurai and in large merchant families during the Edo period (1600–1868), but in many cases, it was the wife who was responsible for managing the household affairs (family budget). This arrangement was maintained from the Meiji period (1868–1912) onward by families in the middle class and above. It is the husband who controls the purse strings in the West, but in Japan it is considered a disgrace for the man of the house to meddle too much in affairs concerning the family budget.

For the common people, there was no superior or inferior ranking in a husband and wife relationship. They both worked together and the wife was additionally responsible for housework and child care. Whether or not the man wears the pants in the house or is henpecked depends on who wields power in the household, but basically it is the wife who determines how much to spend on daily expenses and how much to put into savings.

Question　なぜ, 外国人が箸を使うとびっくりするのですか?

Answer

　確かに, 外国人と食事に行って, 上手に箸を使っているのを見ると, つい「箸の使い方が上手ですね」と聞いてしまいます。

　日本人は自分たちの文化は特殊だと思い込みがちです。箸は中国でも, 韓国でも, 東南アジアでも, いろんな国で使われていることを忘れてしまっているようです。

　それに中華料理が世界で, 日本料理とは比較にならないぐらい, 確たる地位を占めていることも, つい忘れがちです。

　世界のちょっとした都市には, 日本料理店はなくても中国料理店は必ずあり, 中産階級以上の欧米人では, 中華料理の席で箸のマナーを心得ているのは当然とさえ言われている, と聞いて赤面します。

　箸の使い方だけではなく, 日本人は日本語をしゃべる外国人に, 「日本語がお上手ですね」とも言います。これも, 日本語は特殊な言語で, 外国人には覚えるのは難しいものと思い込んでいるところがあるからです。

　箸の使い方が世界では常識であるように, 日本に来る外国の人なら, それなりに日本語については勉強をしてきている人も多いということも, 肝に銘じるべきでしょう。

Q Why are the Japanese so surprised to see non-Japanese use chopsticks?

A When a Japanese and a non-Japanese dine together, and when the Japanese notices that the non-Japanese is able to use chopsticks well, a comment inevitably made by the Japanese is, "You use chopsticks very well."

The Japanese think that their culture is totally unique. They tend to forget that chopsticks are also used in many other countries such as China, Korea and Southeast Asia.

They also tend to forget that Chinese food is highly regarded, even more so than Japanese food that the two cannot even begin to be compared.

It makes the Japanese blush to hear that although a Japanese restaurant may not exist anywhere in a relatively large city, a Chinese restaurant is bound to exist somewhere and that Americans belonging to the middle class and above regard knowing how to use chopsticks properly as only natural.

This phenomenon is not only directed toward the use of chopsticks, but also to non-Japanese who speak Japanese. They are often told, "You speak Japanese very well." The Japanese are under the impression that their language is unique, to the point of being very difficult for non-Japanese to learn.

This is something the Japanese must always keep in mind, that in the same way chopsticks are commonly used throughout the world, many people from other countries come to Japan having studied some Japanese.

Question　なぜ，日本人には左利きが少ないのですか?

Answer

　　日本では，少なくとも昭和20年代までは左利きの人は，「ぎっちょ」と呼ばれて差別されていました。そのために子供のうちに左利きを右利きに直してしまっていたのです。

　　利き手に違いが出る理由は，医学的には，どちらかの側の大脳半球の運動野が，他の側よりも発達しているからだそうですが，一般的には，体の左側を支配する右脳が発達している人，つまり左利きの人は，全体の10%程度という少数派です。

　　日本の社会で，その少数派の左利きの人に対して，右手を使うように強制してきた大きな理由として，漢字の書き方がそもそも右手で書くようにできていることが挙げられます。従って，左利きの子供は，まずは箸を持つ手を右にすることから始まって，右手で文字を書くように矯正されてきたのです。

　　また，稲刈りや草刈りに用いられてきた鎌の刃は，すべて右手で使うように付けられていて，左手では非常に使いにくいものでした。ですから「左利きの娘は嫁に行けない」という農村の言い伝えもありました。

　　利き手は経験や学習で直ると言われますが，現代では，昔のように無理やりに左利きを直そうすることはなくなりましたので，左手で箸を持つ人，漢字を書く人も見かけるようになりました。

Q Why are there so few left-handed people in Japan?

A In Japan, at least until the mid 1940s, left-handed people were called *gitcho*, a degrading term for "left handed" and were discriminated against. Many left-handed people when children were made to switch to their right hand.

Medically speaking, which hand one uses is determined by the motor cortex in the brain's hemisphere that is dominant over the other hemisphere. In general, left-handed people have a dominant right motor cortex, which directs the left side of the body. They are a minority comprising approximately 10% of the overall population.

A major reason why the minority left-handed people were forced to switch to their right hand in Japanese society is that Kanji was created to be written with the right hand. Left-handed children were corrected by making them, first of all, hold the brush in their right hand and then having them write the characters with their right hand.

The blade of a sickle used for reaping rice is made for right-hand convenience that a left-handed person would find awkward to use. There was a saying in the farming villages that a left-handed girl would have almost no prospects of marriage.

It is said that left-handedness can be corrected by practice and training. Compared to before, left-handed people are not forcibly made to switch to their right hand. One now comes across people using chopsticks and writing Kanji with their left hand.

Question なぜ，耳が大きいとほめられるのですか？

Answer

耳たぶが大きい耳を，日本では「福耳」と言います。そして「福耳の人はお金持ちになれる」と言われてきました。

これはそもそも仏陀の姿から来ています。伝説によれば，仏陀は生まれた時には，指には水掻きがあり，頭には突起があり，足の裏には車輪がつき，耳が異常に大きく伸びていたそうです。そして仏教では，耳は神の声を聴く，自然の啓示を聴くものとして特に尊ばれていました。

その仏陀は今では穏やかで神秘的な姿形となっていますが，比較的に大きな耳はそのままです。ですから，その仏の耳のような福々しい耳を持つことは，幸運の印なのです。

また，日本人になじみのある七福神と言われる7人の神様がいますが，この神様たちもいずれも大きな耳をしています。七福神は様々な幸運を人にもたらす縁起のいい神様たちです。大黒天は金運の神様です。

このことから，日本では耳が大きい人には幸運が訪れるという俗信が伝えられ続けてきたのです。

「聖」（神聖な）とか「聡」（聡明な）などいい意味の文字は耳へんであることも，耳の大事さを表しているのかもしれません。

Q Why are people complimented on having big ears?

A Big earlobes in Japanese are called *fukumimi*. It is said that people with big earlobes have the potential to become rich.

This term comes from the figure of Buddha. According to legend, Buddha was born with webbed fingers, a protuberance on his head, wheels on the soles of his feet, and extraordinarily long ears. The ears were revered in Buddhism because ears serve to hear the voice of god as well as natural revelations.

Buddha now assumes a peaceful and a mystical pose, but his relatively large ears remain the same. Having the same kind of fleshy ears as Buddha indicates good luck.

There are seven gods of good luck familiar to the Japanese called Shichifukujin and all of them have big ears. Shichifukujin are auspicious gods bestowing a variety of good luck to people. Daikokuten is a god that bestows good luck with money.

The folk belief that people with big ears will be favored with good luck has continued stemming from the above reasons.

The kanji character for words with favorable meanings such as "sacred," "sacredness," "wise," "wisdom" all contain the ear radical, perhaps depicting the importance that was accorded to the ear.

Question　なぜ，日本人には肥満の人が少ないのですか？

Answer　かなり西洋風の食事が多くなったとはいえ，日本の食卓の基本は，やはり和食です。

　アメリカ，ヨーロッパの一般家庭の食事に比べますと，アメリカ人やフランス人が，1日に約3500カロリーの食事をとっているのに，日本人は約2600カロリーです。しかも，動物性食品の摂取量は，日本人は欧米人の半分から，多くて5分の3です。和食は基本的にかなり食べても太らない食事なのです。

　もちろん日本でも太っていることを気にして，ダイエットに挑む人が後を断ちません。しかし，欧米人の肥満というのは，日本人には考えられないほどのものすごさですから，外国人の目から見ると，日本人の肥満はささやかな程度に見えるのでしょう。

　肥満は遺伝によるという説もあるそうですが，証明はされていず，むしろ，肥満した親がいる家庭の食事の環境が，子供も肥満にしていきやすい，というのが実情ではないかと思われます。

　太平洋戦争後，食生活が豊かになって，日本人の中にも肥満の人が急激に増えたことは事実ですが，最近は男性の肥満者の数は横ばいです。女性のほうはむしろ，痩せすぎの人が目立つようになりました。

Q Why are there so few overweight Japanese?

A Although Western foods are eaten with great frequency, the food served on the table in Japan is basically Japanese.

Compared to food served in the ordinary home in the United States and Europe, the Japanese consume approximately 2,600 calories a day as opposed to the Americans and the French who consume approximately 3,500 calories a day. The intake of animal foods by the Japanese ranges from half to three fifths at most, to that of Westerners. Basically, large amounts of Japanese food can be eaten without gaining weight.

But many Japanese think they are overweight and there is no end to the people who go on a diet. But being overweight by Western standards greatly exceeds what the Japanese regard as being overweight and this may perhaps be the reason why Westerners regard overweight Japanese as not really being overweight.

There is a theory that obesity is determined by one's genes although there is nothing to prove it is so. It is more likely that children have a tendency to become obese if they grow up in an environment where the food served is prepared by an obese parent.

It is a fact that after World War II, the number of overweight Japanese has rapidly increased because of a rich diet. The number of overweight men has recently leveled off, but the number of underweight women, on the other hand, has markedly increased.

Question　なぜ，日本人は長生きなのですか？

Answer　厚生省の調査によれば，1995年の日本人の平均寿命は男性が76.36年，女性が82.84年で，男女とも世界一になっています。戦争直後の1947年の平均寿命は，男性が50.06年，女性が53.96年でしたから，その後の伸びは経済発展以上の驚異的な伸びと言わざるをえません。

　その理由は簡単ではありませんが，1つは食生活の改善です。

　世界の食生活は欧米先進国の「低炭水化物，高動物性蛋白質，高脂肪」と，発展途上国の「高炭水化物，低動物性蛋白質，低脂肪」の2つに大きく分けられます。

　日本は経済発展によって発展途上国型から先進国型に向かったのですが，米中心の「和食」の伝統のおかげで，栄養学的に見てバランスのとれた理想的なところに落ち着いたのです。

　第2の理由は，医学の発展により，これまで日本人の三大死因であった，結核，肺炎，胃腸炎がすべて克服されたことです。

　そしてもう1つ，保険医療制度の確立も大きな要因です。これにより，だれもが気軽に病院に行って，治療が受けられるようになったのです。

Q Why do the Japanese live so long?

A According to a survey carried out by the Ministry of Health and Welfare, the average life expectancy of the Japanese in 1995 was 76.36 years for men and 82.84 years for women, the longest in the world for both men and women. The average life expectancy immediately following the war in 1947 was 50.06 years for men and 53.96 years for women, marking a remarkable gain that even exceeded economic growth.

It is not easy to come up with reasons for this remarkable gain in life expectancy, but one of them is the improved diet.

Diet throughout the world can be broadly classified under two large headings. The first is the diet of the advanced nations of the West which is low in carbohydrates and high in animal protein and fat. The other is the diet of the developing countries which is high in carbohydrates and low in animal protein and fat.

Economic development enabled Japan to evolve from a developing country to an advanced nation, but owing to its traditional Japanese diet of rice as its staple food, its diet stabilized at an ideal nutritional balance.

The second reason is the advancement of medical science. There are now cures for tuberculosis, pneumonia and gastroenteritis, which until recently were the three main causes of death of the Japanese.

The third is the establishment of a health insurance system which is an important factor that enables anyone to receive affordable medical care anytime.

Question　なぜ，八重歯だとかわいいと言われるのですか？

Answer

　今の日本でも歯並びを矯正する人は，非常に多くなりました。やはり白く形のそろった歯が整然と並んでいるほうがいいと思うのは，日本でも同様です。しかし，日本に歯医者さんが多くなってからも，歯並びを矯正するという習慣は，あまり広まりませんでした。費用もかかることから，庶民には手の届かないことでもありました。

　日本人の歯には，反っ歯と八重歯が多いと言われています。反っ歯は上の前歯が前下方に突き出ています。そして，八重歯というのは，八重桜の花びらが重なりあっているように，歯が別の歯のわきに重なるように生えることを言います。特に犬歯が前に出ていたりすると，ドラキュラの歯を思い起こしたりしますから，欧米人に嫌われることはよくわかります。

　しかし，日本人はこの歯並びの不ぞろいなところに，自然な愛敬を認めてきました。確かに日本人の，能面のような表情の起伏の乏しい顔には，八重歯がちょっとのぞくことによって，愛らしい表情が生まれてきます。

　ホクロも同様です。欧米ではホクロは皮膚の異常と受け取られますから，手術で取ってしまいますが，日本ではかなり大きなものはともかく，小さなものは「カワイイ！」と見られます。やはり，彫りが深くない日本人の顔では，八重歯同様に，愛敬を示すアクセントになるのです。

Q Why are double teeth considered charming?

A Many people in Japan now have their teeth straightened. The Japanese also consider white, regularly positioned teeth to be attractive. However, even when dentists increased in number, the practice of straightening teeth was not widespread. Because of the high cost, it was beyond the means of the ordinary people.

It is said that the Japanese have a high incidence of projecting and double teeth. Projecting teeth refers to the upper front teeth projecting down in an overbite. Double teeth refers to a tooth growing in a position so that it overlaps along the side of another tooth like the petal of a double flowering cherry blossom. Why it is disliked by Westerners is understandable especially when the canine tooth emerges to the front and takes on a resemblance to Dracula.

The Japanese, however, see a natural charm in irregularly positioned teeth. The Japanese face is like a bland Noh mask devoid of expression. A glimpse of a double tooth adds charm and appeal to this bland facial expression.

The same goes for moles. Westerners think of moles as a skin abnormality and have them surgically removed. Unless it is very large, the Japanese think of little moles as being cute. Moles, like double teeth, serve to accent the shallow features of the Japanese face.

Question　なぜ, 日本のコメディアンは相手方をあんなにひっぱたくのですか?

Answer

　特に漫才で見かけるシーンだと思います。そのような漫才を「どつき漫才」と言っていますが, 多くなったのは, 1970年代のテレビの漫才ブームの時からです。

　漫才には「ぼけ」の役と「つっこみ」の役という役割の分担があり, その絶妙の掛け合いで笑わせます。「ぼけ」はとぼけ役,「つっこみ」は賢そうに話を持ち掛ける役です。

　この2人の対比を強調するために, 相手の頭を掌でポンとたたいたり, ハリセンという紙を折り畳んだもので顔を引っぱたいたり, 中には飛び蹴りで相手をすっ飛ばしたりするのです。

　暴力とかセックスの場面に対して厳しい規制のあるアメリカでは, このような漫才のどつきが暴力的に見えるのだと思います。

　しかし, 親しい間柄でよく「何, 言ってるんだい, 君」などと言って, ドンと相手の背中をたたいたりすることはありませんか。女性が「まあ, いやだわ」と言って, ポンと相手をたたくこともあります。

　ですから, ある程度の「どつき」は親愛の情の表れということもできますし, 別にけんかをしているわけではないどつきあいは, 一種の気合みたいなもので, 爽快さをおぼえることもあります。もちろん程度の問題ですが――。

Q Why do Japanese comedians slap and hit their partner?

A This is particularly true in *manzai* or a stand-up comedy act. This type of slapstick comedy called *dotsuki manzai* was at its height in popularity during the *manzai* boom on TV in the 1970s.

Manzai roles are divided into the *boke* or "not with it" role, and the *tsukkomi* or the "clever" role. Their rapid-fire exchange draws laughter for their wit and humor. The *boke* plays dumb and the *tsukkomi* is the know-it-all who carries the verbal exchange along.

To emphasize the contrast between the *tsukkomi* and the *boke*, the *boke* would be hit on the head with the palm of the hand or slapped in the face with a paper rolled up in an accordion-like fashion. There are some who are even kicked and sent flying.

The United States places strict restrictions on violence and sex scenes, and Americans may find slapstick comedy like the above to be a little too violent.

But people who know each other well might sometimes slap the other on the back with something like, "Hey! What do you think you're saying!" Women might say, while lightly slapping the other on the back, "Oh, how awful!"

To some extent, slapping and hitting is a show of affection for the other and when it is not a fight, it is a type of encouragement that is not meant to offend, but of course it all depends on the degree.

Question なぜ，日本の医者は患者に真実を伝えないのですか？

Answer

　アメリカでは医療は「サービス」であり，患者は客という認識で通っているようですが，日本では医者は「先生」であり，患者はその先生のお世話になっている，という認識を持っている人がまだまだ多いようです。医者を信頼することが患者の義務だと思っている人もいます。

　ですから，医者に治療のことを問いただすなんてことはめったにしませんし，医者のほうも，なかなか患者に専門的な治療の詳細を説明して，いわゆるインフォームド・コンセントを得ようとしないという慣習が続いています。

　また，日本人は不必要に事を荒立てることを避けようとする国民ですから，医者の治療に疑問を感じても，医療訴訟を起こすことはアメリカに比べると非常に少ないのです。

　アメリカでは，患者に治療の具体的な内容を伝え，患者の了解のもとに治療をしていかないと，仮に訴訟が起こったときに，医者が敗訴してしまうそうですから，医者は自衛策のために患者に治療内容を伝えているとも言えます。

　最近は日本でも，医者にきちんとした治療内容の説明を求める人が多くなりました。がん告知に関しても，ある新聞の調査で，60％以上の人が，告知してほしいと望んでいます。

Q Why don't Japanese doctors tell patients the truth?

A In the United States, medical care is considered to be a service and the patients consider themselves to be customers. In Japan, many people consider the doctor to be the master and the patients as people who are indebted to the master for his or her services. There are people who feel that patients are obligated to trust the doctor implicitly.

In Japan, the practice of questioning the doctor is rarely done and the doctor also does not attempt to explain in detail the kind of treatment that will be administered. Not obtaining an informed consensus from the patient is still prevalent.

Also, the Japanese are a people who try to avoid making unnecessary waves. Even when they harbor doubts about the treatment given by the doctor, it is very rare, unlike in the United States, that they would take legal action against the doctor.

In the United States, the patient is informed specifically on matters concerning method of treatment and the patient's consent is obtained before treatment is undertaken, otherwise the doctor would be in a vulnerable position to lose in the event a lawsuit is filed. Informing patients on the details of treatment is also a measure taken for the doctor's own self-protection.

Presently in Japan, more and more people are demanding a clear and detailed explanation concerning method of treatment. According to a newspaper survey, more than 60% of the people want to be told if they have cancer.

Question　なぜ，日本は臓器移植に消極的なのですか？

Answer

　　死後，人間は成仏して「仏」になると，多くの日本人は考えています。ですから，葬儀で人々は死者の冥福を祈り，無事に「成仏」してくれることを願います。

　　成仏という言葉は，浄土教系の仏教から出てきた思想ですが，これに儒教的な思想が加わって，遺骨を埋葬し，墓を建て，家に仏壇を作って位牌を置き，身近に霊を祀るという日本人の一般的な習わしができています。

　　従って，日本人の多くは，人は死んでも仏になるまで，霊は肉体の周辺をさまよっていると考えています。ですから，まだ呼吸をしたり，血が体の中を巡ったりしているのに，脳死で人間の死を判定し，臓器を取り出すなどして，肉体を傷つけることには，大きな抵抗があるのです。

　　また，五体満足な体は父母からもらったものであり，たとえ死後とは言え，体を傷つけることはもってのほか，という考えもありました。

　　しかし近年は，これまでの日本の宗教的な背景に縛られずに，脳死を人の死とすることに抵抗がない人も増えてきました。それに伴って，生前にドナーとしての登録をして，自分の死後，自分の体を世の中に役立てたいという人も多くなっています。

Q Why are so few organ transplants carried out in Japan?

A Many Japanese believe that a person achieves *jōbutsu* or a spiritual awakening and becomes a Buddha after death. At funerals, people pray for *jōbutsu* and for the happiness of the departed person in the next world.

Jōbutsu is a concept derived from a form of the Jodo sect of Buddhism which incorporates Confucian concepts such as: burying the remains, making a grave and placing the memorial tablet on the family altar—all forming the basis of the Japanese custom of enshrining the dead in close proximity.

Many Japanese believe that the spirit of the dead linger around the vicinity of the body before becoming a Buddha. The Japanese have strong feelings against the idea of damaging the body to remove the internal organs based on the criteria of judging a person's death as brain death when a person is still breathing and when blood is still circulating throughout the body.

Another reason is that the Japanese think it is inexcusable to damage, even after death, a healthy and normal body that is inherited intact from one's parents.

Recently, more and more people not bound by the religious traditions of Japan have come to accept brain death as actual death. Accompanying this trend is the increase in the number of people who register to become donors hoping that their contribution after death will be of some benefit to society.

Question なぜ, ファッション雑誌はモデルに外国人を使うのですか?

Answer

　確かに「With」「MORE」「FRAU」など, ハイセンスを売りものにしているファッション雑誌には, 外国人のモデルが多く登場します。しかし「ViVi」や「CanCam」などのように, 身近なファッションを売りものにしている雑誌では, 日本人モデルがほとんどなのです。

　この理由は, ハイセンスな雑誌は, 各国のブランドの服の紹介が多いわけですが, このような服は欧米人の体型に合うように作られていて, また特に, 髪の色や目の色が金髪や青い目に合うような色使いになっているので, 外国人が着たほうが引き立つという利点があるのです。

　ですから, 読者に対する親近感という点では, 日本人モデルにしたいという要求もあるのですが, ハイセンスなところを強調するということで, 外国人モデルが多くなっています。

　確かに, 戦後に次々と出されたファッション雑誌では, モデルは欧米人, あるいはハーフでなくっちゃ, という時代もありましたが, 今や西欧人の体型に見劣りをしない日本人のモデルがたくさんいて, 世界でも大活躍をしている時代ですから, 雑誌の内容に応じて, 外国人, 日本人のモデルが使い分けられていくわけです。

Q Why do fashion magazines use foreign models?

A Many foreign models appear in fashion magazines such as *With*, *MORE* and *FRAU* that cater to high fashion, and many Japanese models appear in more down-to-earth fashion magazines such as *ViVi* and *CanCam*.

Designer clothes of many countries appear in high-fashion magazines giving foreign models an advantage. The clothes are made to fit Western proportions and the colors are coordinated to complement light hair color and eye color to bring out a contrast, making clothes look all the finer on foreign models.

To bring these fashions closer to home to the Japanese, there are requests to use Japanese models, but foreign models are used much more frequently when the emphasis is on high fashion.

When fashion magazines began to be published in succession after the war, there was a period when the models were required to be either Western or a racial mixture of part Japanese and part Western. There are now many Japanese models with proportions on par with that of Westerners who are actively modeling on the world stage. The time will come when the contents of these fashion magazines will be adapted to accommodate both foreign and Japanese models.

Question　**なぜ，テレビのアイドルはあんなに歌が下手なのですか？**

Answer

　日本では，歌が上手だからといってアイドルになれるわけではありません。ところがアイドルになりさえすれば，いくら下手でも歌わせてもらえるし，ドラマにも出してもらえます。

　太平洋戦争後，映画が圧倒的な人気であった1950～60年代までは，映画俳優の中からアイドルが続々と生まれました。吉永小百合，石原裕次郎などがそうです。歌も歌っているうちに，結構，聞けるようになりました。

　その後，1970年代から80年代にかけて，テレビの歌番組が全盛となり，少々歌が下手でもテレビの威力で，可愛くて視聴者受けすれば一気に人気が出ることから，多くのアイドルが歌手としてデビューしてきました。その中には聞くに堪えない歌を歌うアイドルが多かったのですが，山口百恵のように，歌の実力，演技の実力も備えたアイドルが登場することもありました。

　1980年代後半からは，歌番組は人気がなくなり，アイドルの条件は厳しくなりました。可愛いだけではだめですし，歌だけでもアイドルにはなれません。1996年になって人気急上昇の安室奈美恵のように，歌やダンスのレッスンを重ねてきた上で，ルックスも個性的という実力派が，アイドルの条件になりそうです。

Q Why can't idol singers appearing on TV sing?

A In Japan, singing ability is not a prerequisite for becoming a popular singer. If one makes it as an idol, opportunities open up to sing in public and to act in TV dramas regardless of the ability.

The period from 1950–60 after the end of World War II marked a surge of overwhelming popularity for movies. Idols from the ranks of movie actors and actresses appeared in succession such as YOSHINAGA Sayuri and ISHIHARA Yujiro. Their songs actually came over quite well the more they sang and the more one became used to their singing.

TV hit parade programs were at the height of their popularity from the 1970s to the 1980s. Many of these idols debuted as singers through the power of TV even if their singing left much to be desired. They became instant stars if they had the right looks and an image that went over well with the viewers. The singing of many of these young pop singers was unbearable, but there were a few, however, such as YAMAGUCHI Momoe who were blessed with the ability to both sing and act.

These TV hit parade programs lost their popularity in the latter half of the 1980s and the qualifications for becoming an idol became stringent. It was not enough just to look cute or to sing well. The qualification for becoming an idol in 1996 is someone like the popular and rising star, AMURO Namie, who has built up her career by taking music and dancing lessons and who is endowed with both unique looks and real talent.

Question　なぜ，駅や電車のアナウンスはあんなにうるさいのですか?

Answer

　　日本人は基本的に世話好きです。ですから，「お忘れもののないようにお降りください」「白線の内側をお歩きください」などなど，いずれも親切心からのアナウンスだ，と解釈していただきたいと思います。

　　しかし，このようなアナウンスは，なくてもいい感じもします。「押し合わずにご乗車ください」などと，乗客の品性をまったく信用していないようなアナウンスもあり，日本人の中にもうんざりしている人がたくさんいます。

　　乗り物に乗る以上，乗客個々人の責任で気をつければいいことですから，せいぜい，到着した駅名，次の駅の名前，乗り換えの案内ぐらいをアナウンスをするだけで済みそうなのに，なぜか，少々おせっかいすぎるのです。どうもここに，サービスという名目のもとに世間の非難や攻撃を回避しようとする日本人の知恵がありそうです。

　　今はPL（製造物責任）ということが問われている時代です。電子レンジにネコを入れてはいけないと，説明書に書いてなかった——というので，メーカーが事故の責任を負わされたという笑い話に近い話がありますが，サービスの世界も同様ではないでしょうか。上のようななくもがなのアナウンスでも，何か起こったときに，あんなに注意を促していたのに，というための責任逃れの手段のようにも思えます。

Q Why are announcements made at stations and on trains such a nuisance?

A The Japanese are basically a people who like to do things for others. Announcements such as, "When leaving, please make sure to take all your belongings with you," or "Please walk within the area marked by the white line," can all be interpreted as looking out for the welfare of the other.

However, these announcements perhaps can just as well not exist. Announcements such as, "Please enter without pushing," can be interpreted an outright distrust of the character of the passengers that many Japanese also find too much to take.

Responsibility should be taken by each individual to look out for themselves while commuting. Pertinent announcements such as the name of the station one has arrived at, the name of the next station and instructions for transferring should be all that is necessary, but there invariably are some announcements that go a little too far. Lurking under the pretext of service lies the tactic of the Japanese to avoid coming under fire from the public.

This is an age when PL (product liability) is being called to account for damages. There is the not-too-funny story about a manufacturer being held responsible for the accident that occurred for not stating specifically in the instruction that cats should not be put in the microwave oven. This is also true in the service sector. Unnecessary announcements like the above might be a means of avoiding responsibility should anything occur to provide a pretext of, "after all, we did warn you."

Question なぜ，日本の警察官はあんなに紳士的なのですか？

Answer

　日本の警察は，明治憲法の下では，内務省に所属する国家の行政組織であり，警察官はすべて国の官吏でした。

　1954年に制定された現行の警察法では，警察は国の警察機関である警察庁と，警視庁をはじめとした都道府県の警察機関の2つに分けられました。そして，実際の警察としての市民生活の中での活動は，都道府県警察が担当しています。

　現行の警察法では日常の警察活動は，社会秩序の維持や犯罪防止など，消極的な範囲に限定されています。明治憲法下で持っていた命令や強制の権力は警察官にはありません。警察官が権力的な手段を行使する場合には，現行犯としての逮捕を認められている場合をのぞき，きちんとした書類が必要です。

　もちろん，現行犯逮捕として凶暴な犯人にピストルを1発，発射することもあるでしょうが，後で，それが妥当であったかどうかが厳しく検討されます。

　また，警察が民事上の問題に干渉することはできませんし，警察官は日本でいちばん厳格な規制を強いられている職業だと言えます。ですから，警察官は日本でいちばん紳士的なのです。

Q Why are the Japanese police such gentlemen?

A Under the Meiji Constitution, the Japanese police was an administrative organ of the state under the control of the prewar Ministry of Home Affairs. All policemen were government officials of the state.

The current police law which was enacted in 1954 divided the police into two organizations: the National Police Agency under the state; and the Metropolitan Police Department in Tokyo and all the prefectures in addition to Hokkaido, Osaka and Kyoto. The prefectural police as well as the police of Hokkaido, Osaka and Kyoto are responsible for police work concerning the inhabitants.

The scope of the present police law limits police work to passive involvement such as to maintain social order and to prevent crime. The mandate held by the police and the authoritative power it had under the Meiji Constitution no longer exists. When the police exercise their rights, they are required to have the proper papers ready, except for arrests when warranted of people caught in the act of committing a crime.

The police may on occasions fire a shot at a brutal criminal caught in the act of committing a crime, but they would later come under harsh scrutiny as to whether the shot fired was appropriate or not.

The police are not allowed to interfere in civil issues and as an occupation, they are subjected to the most stringent regulations in Japan. This is why the police are the most gentlemanly in Japan.

Question なぜ, エレベーター・ガールがいるのですか?

Answer

　　日本にエレベーターができたのは1890年(明治23年),浅草公園内にあった凌雲閣という12階の建物だったそうですが,その後,百貨店などに続々と登場してきます。

　　当時は自動ではありませんから,エレベーター・ガールがついて運転をしていたのは当然です。女性の花形職業でもありました。若い女性のやさしい声で案内されてエレベーターに乗り込むのですから,客をいい気分にさせるサービスでもあります。そのサービスが今もしっかり残っているのです。

　　これを無駄なことと見るかどうかは,駅の過剰なアナウンスを無駄と見るか,ということとも関連してきそうですが,乗り込もうとして突然閉まるエレベーターのドアにまごついて,けがをする年寄りや子供がいるかもしれないことを考えると,あながちエレベーター・ガールの存在が無用とも言えません。

　　最近は自動のエレベーターに慣れた客が多くなりましたから,1階で乗る客に対してだけ案内をすることが多くなりましたし,無人の場合もあり,次第にエレベーター・ガールが消えていくことは間違いありませんが——。

Q Why are elevator girls necessary?

A The first elevator was installed in 1890 in a twelve story building called Ryōunkaku located in Asakusa Park. Later, elevators were installed one after another in department stores.

The elevator girls operated the controls because the elevators were not automatic. This was considered to be a glamor occupation for women in those days. Being in an elevator guided by a young woman's sweet voice is a service enough to make any customer happy, and this service has endured to the present.

This may appear to be a useless service, but a connection can be made as to whether the excessive announcements made at train stations are useless or not. The service performed by elevator girls may not be superfluous, considering that an elderly person or a child, upon entering the elevator, might sustain injuries at the sudden closure of the elevator door.

There are many customers now who are used to automatic elevators, and there are many places where guidance is given only to customers who get on at the first floor. There are many unmanned elevators and it will surely not be long before elevator girls will become a remembrance of the past.

5

日本の
会社の
ふしぎ

Puzzling Features of
the Company
in Japan

Question　**なぜ，就職や出世に学歴がものを言うのですか？**

Answer　　科学技術の発達により産業は高度になり，次々と専門職を必要としてきましたので，そういう仕事ができる人たちを育てるために，高い教育水準，つまり学歴が必要となったのは，決して日本だけではないと思います。

　　日本では現在，義務教育の小学校・中学校を卒業した後，大半が高校に行き，さらに大学にも行きたいと望むのですが，大学に入ることができるのは1994年でも，高校卒業生の半分以下の43.3％です。

　　そうなると，多くが浪人あるいは就職を余儀無くされるわけですから，とにかく，どんな大学でも入れればいいというわけで受験戦争に巻き込まれていきます。しかも，大企業への就職率がいい大学に入ろうとすると，もう，小学校の時から勉強，勉強です。

　　しかも，日本では会社側に，採用した人間を会社内で優秀な会社人間として育て上げるといった傾向がありましたから，いい大学に優秀な人材がいる──と短絡に考え，学歴を重視した採用をしています。

　　また有名大学の出身者は，他の会社でも官庁でも活躍をしていることから，企業はその人脈を利用することも考えています。

Q Why does academic background count in employment and in promotions?

A Industry has become highly technical with the advancement of scientific technology, and jobs requiring specialization have sprung up one after another. Japan is not the only country that finds a high educational level, or in other words, an advanced educational background necessary to train a work force able to tackle these highly specialized jobs.

Most students in Japan go on to high school after finishing compulsory education in the elementary and junior high school levels. Many have a desire to continue on to university level, but those able to make it into universities in 1994 made up 43.3% or less than half of all high school graduates.

Many of those not making it into universities have another try at the entrance examination or join the work force. Getting admitted to a well-known university lies behind this stiff entrance examination competition. Admittance to a good university where a high percentage of its graduates enter large, well-known corporations requires intense studying from the elementary school level on.

The company trains the new employees to become valuable assets to the company and hence, the prevailing reasoning that qualified workers can be had from good universities and the importance placed on academic background in hiring.

Graduates from well-known universities are conspicuous in other companies and in the government. Many businesses eye to make use of graduates from well-known universities because of the financial and political links that they share.

Question なぜ，日本では長い休暇がとれないのですか？

Answer

　日本の年間休日数は1993年で124日です。アメリカは132日，イギリスは136日，フランスは138日，ドイツは145日です。欧米に比べてまだ少ないですが，働き過ぎの日本と非難されていた時に比べると，かなり休暇が多くなりました。しかし，フランスの4週間，ドイツの5週間といった長期の休暇となると，日本ではまだまだです。

　長期休暇が取れない理由としては，「自分が休むと同僚に迷惑がかかる」ということがいちばん多いようです。また，高度経済成長期には，「会社に行っていないと取り残されそうな気がする」と思った人もいました。人をこういう意識にさせるのは日本の会社のシステムがいちばんの原因です。

　日本の会社は，部，課，係など，上下に組織が細かく分けられています。そこにはそれぞれ，そのセクションの責任者とその部下がいて，いっしょに仕事をしていますし，しかも，社員が自分の会社を「うちの会社」と呼ぶといった家族主義的な雰囲気ですから，自分だけが長期に休むことは気がひけるのです。

　雇用は会社と自分との個人契約である，というアメリカ社会のような意識がもっと育たないと，仕事の他のライフワークを，日本人はなかなか見つけ出すことができないかもしれません。

Q Why can't Japanese workers take long vacations?

A The number of days off taken by the Japanese in 1993 was 124 days. Americans took 132 days off, the English 136 days off, the French 138 days off and the Germans 145 days off. This figure is still less than the other Western nations but more compared to when Japan was criticized for being a nation of workaholics. Japan still has a long way to go when it comes to taking long vacations like the 4 weeks taken in France and the 5 weeks taken in Germany.

The reason most often cited for being unable to take a long vacation is, "being absent will inconvenience one's colleagues." In the period of high economic growth, there were others who cited, "afraid of being left behind if absent from the office." The way Japanese companies are run is the foremost reason why the company weighs heavily on the workers' mind.

Japanese companies are closely divided into a vertical-tiered structure of *bu* (department) at the top and *ka* and *kakari* (sections) below *bu*. Each division is run by a person in charge who works together with the people under him or her. The company is like a big family and the employees call the company "our company." They tend to feel uncomfortable about being the only one to take a long vacation.

Unless the way American companies view employment as a personal contract between the company and an individual is not fostered, the Japanese will find it difficult to find another interest or a "life work" other than company work to occupy them throughout their lifetime.

Question なぜ，会社は女性をもっと活躍させないのですか？

Answer

産業によって差がありますが，サービス業，金融・不動産業，卸・小売業などでは，女性労働者の比率が，1994年には50%を超えています。全産業では38.8%（総務庁「労働力調査年報」）です。パートタイムで働く人たちも含めると80%前後になります。

しかし，1993年以降，日本経済は低成長期に入っており，女性の就職への門は非常に狭くなっています。

日本の会社の多くは終身雇用制度をとっていますから，いつ結婚してやめていくかわからず，出産，育児と，男性よりも休暇が多くなる女性は敬遠されるのです。

1986年施行の「男女雇用機会均等法」で，男女の平等の権利が保障され，企業にもその責任が求められていますが，これには罰則規定はありません。

しかし，女性の意識の変革で，管理職につく女性も増え，これまで男だけの職場と思われた建築現場や，大型トラックの運転などの世界にも，かなりの女性が進出してきました。

育児休暇制度や保育施設なども社会的に整ってきましたので，女性が活躍する場は急激に広がるでしょう。

Q Why don't companies make more use of women workers?

A There are differences depending on the industry, but the percentage of women employees in 1994 was more than 50% in industries such as service, finance, real estate, and wholesale and retail. According to the annual manpower survey by the Management and Coordination Agency, women employees accounted for 38.8% in all industries and overall women workers reached a high of about 80% when part-timers were included.

However, in 1993 and thereafter, work opportunities for women became extremely limited due to the period of low economic growth of the Japanese economy.

The lifetime employment system of Japanese companies make many companies hesitate to employ women workers for fear they would quit the company upon marriage and because of their tendency to take more days off than men due to childbirth and child care.

The Equal Employment Opportunity Law enacted in 1986 guarantees equal rights for both men and women. Companies are expected to follow this ruling but there are no provisions for penalization.

However, women's views regarding work has undergone a change and there are now more women in administrative posts, as well as in fields such as construction site work which was formerly men only, and large-size truck drivers.

The child care leave system has been implemented and day-care facilities have been upgraded enabling more and more women to expand their work horizons.

Question なぜ，女子社員だけが制服を着なければならない会社があるのですか?

Answer 　女性はおしゃれが好きですから，会社の中の服装が自由であれば，どうしても見栄の張り合いになりかねないところがあります。しかし，そんな無駄なエネルギーを仕事以外のことに使ってもらっては困るというわけで，日本の会社では，会社の中で女子社員に制服を着せるのです——というのも1つの理由ですが，本来は制服には様々な利点が挙げられます。

　デパートなどではだれが店員かが制服で明確ですから，客にとっては便利です。そして，制服を着ている以上，それを着ている人は自分の会社のイメージを損なわないように行動に注意をします。つまり，制服はその会社のCI，動く広告塔でもあるわけです。また，制服であれば，日常，着る物に余計な費用をかけなくても済みます。

　また制服は女性に限られているのではなく，工場などでは制服を義務づけているところがほとんどです。

　それに，日本の男性ビジネスマンは，外国人の目から見て「どぶネズミ」みたいだと言われる地味な色のスーツを着ています。これも制服と言えないこともありませんね。

　おそらく欧米では反発を買うことが多いでしょうが，よく指摘されるように，家族主義的な経営，集団主義的なビジネス活動という日本の会社組織の中では，あまり抵抗なく受け入れられているのが制服です。

Q Why do some companies require only women employees to wear uniforms?

A Women love to dress up and there is a risk they would try to outdo one another if they were free to dress as they pleased. Using unnecessary energy on matters unrelated to work would be detrimental to the company, hence the policy that women employees must wear uniforms. But this is only part of the reason. Essentially, there are many advantages to wearing uniforms.

It is convenient for customers to be able to tell at a glance by uniforms who the salesclerks are in a department store. As long as uniforms are worn, the person in uniform would use discretion not to tarnish the company's image. In other words, the uniform is the company's corporate identity and a moving advertisement tower. Also, there is no need to spend on clothes when uniforms are required.

Uniforms are not limited only to women. Most factories require their workers to wear uniforms.

Japanese businessmen in drab suits may look like gutter rats to non-Japanese. These suits can also be regarded as a type of uniform.

Westerners may rebel against wearing uniforms, but uniforms are accepted with little resistance in the often pointed out family-type management and the collective type of business activity in the way Japanese companies are run.

Question **なぜ, 日本の会社では根回しをしないと仕事が進まないのですか?**

Answer

「根回し」とはもともと園芸の言葉で, 大木を移植する前に, 根の回りを掘って, 主根以外の根を切り, 小根を出させて, 移植しやすくすることを言います。

ここから転じて, 正式な会議で決定する前に, あらかじめ関係者の賛成をとりつけて, プランが通るようにすることを言います。

こんなまだるっこしい手順が存在する原因は, 日本の会社のシステムにあります。

日本の会社は, 部, 課, 係など, 細かく上から下に組織化されており, それぞれのセクションには責任者とその部下がいます。そして, そのセクションが, 1つの共同体として仕事を進めていきます。

とにかく, 仕事は同僚, 上役に対する思惑で進めないといけません。個性が強くて, 個人プレーに走る人もいますが, 孤立することが多いようです。必然, 何かいい提案があっても, 前もって周囲, 上司に相談, つまり「根回し」しておかないと, 最終の決定にまで持っていくことができないのです。

役員でも, 日本の会社では即決即断を下せる権限を持った人は少なく, 役員会にかけなければ最終決定できず, やはり根回しをすることが多いのです。

Q Why can't work proceed without *nemawashi* in Japanese companies?

A *Nemawashi* was formerly a gardening term referring to digging around the root of a large tree before transplanting and cutting off the roots except for the main root to induce the little roots to grow to make transplanting easier.

The meaning has shifted to also mean laying the groundwork in advance to get the approval of the people involved in order to get a plan or proposal passed.

This roundabout process exists because of the system in Japanese companies.

Japanese companies are tightly organized in a top-down structure with a *bu* (department) at the top and the sections of *ka* and *kakari* below *bu*. Each division is comprised of a person in charge and subordinates working under the person in charge. Each division carries out its work as a community.

Work must be carried out according to the expectations of one's colleagues and superiors. Those displaying uniqueness and who go their own way usually find themselves isolated from the group. Coming up with a good proposal does not guarantee legitimacy in bringing the proposal to the final decision-making stage. Consultation with one's superiors and all the other people around is necessary, in other words, *nemawashi* must be carried out first.

Very few directors in Japanese companies have the authority to make prompt decisions and snap judgments. It has to be brought before the board of directors before a final decision can be made, and for this, *nemawashi* must often be carried out beforehand.

Question なぜ, 相手を肩書で呼ぶのですか?

Answer

確かに日本人は, 会社の中の相手に対して, 「社長」とか「専務」,「部長」,「課長」など, 相手を仕事上の肩書で呼びます。自分の会社だけではなく, 得意先の相手に対しても, 高い地位の人に対しては, その肩書で呼びます。

これは, 日本の社会は「タテ社会」という構造になっており, 常に上下意識で関係が保たれていることの表れです。

アメリカ人は会社の上役に対しても, 仕事仲間である相手に対してはファースト・ネームで呼びかけますが, 日本では考えられないことです。必ず肩書か,「〜さん」と名字を呼ばなければなりません。課長に対して「一郎さん」などと名前を呼んだら, 失礼なことになります。

また, 家庭の中でも,「あなた」とか, あるいは名前を呼んでいた夫婦が, 子供ができたりすると, 妻は夫を「お父さん」, 夫は妻を「お母さん」と呼ぶようになります。

つまり, そのコミュニティーの中で果たしている役割で相手を呼ぶのです。

自分と相手との関係が明確になる, このような呼び方によって, お互いの立場を認め合うことになりますから, 余計なトラブルも起こりません。日本人が「和」を尊ぶ民族であると言われるゆえんでもあります。

Q Why do the Japanese call the other by title?

A The Japanese call people in their companies by the position they hold such as *shachō* (president), *buchō* (general manager) or *kachō* (manager). People holding high positions not only in their own company, but also in other companies with business ties to their own company are also called by titles.

This stems from the structure of Japanese society based on a pecking order where a superior-inferior vertical relationship in relation to the other is constantly maintained.

In American companies, superiors and inferiors are all on a first name basis which is not done in Japan. In Japan, the other must always be called by a title or by adding *san* (Mr. Ms. Miss) after the surname. Calling one's manager Ichiro-san by adding *san* after his first name is rude.

In the home, a wife would call her husband *anata* (you, dear, darling) or by his first name. After the children are born, she would call him *otōsan* (father) and he would call her *okāsan* (mother).

In other words, the other is called by the role he or she plays in society.

This method of calling by title or by role clarifies the relationship between oneself and the other and brings about an awareness of the position of the other, making unnecessary inconveniences less likely to occur. This is why the Japanese are said to be a people who revere harmony.

Question　なぜ, 仕事で名刺が必要なのですか?

Answer

　　名刺は日本独自のものではなく, 昔, 中国で上位の役人に目下の者が会うときに, 削った竹に名前を書いて相手に渡したことが起源だと言われています。それなのになぜ, 日本人の名刺好きが注目されるのか, その理由には次のことが挙げられます。

　　1つには, 漢字で表す日本人の名前には, 同音語がたくさんあって, 耳で聞いただけでは区別できないことがありますから, 文字で書かれた名刺が非常に便利なのです。

　　例えばナガイ・ヒロシと言っても, ナガイには永井, 長井, 長居があるし, ヒロシには博, 浩, 宏, 弘などたくさんあって, いったいどの組み合わせかということは, 耳では理解できません。

　　それにもう1つ, 日本の社会では, 相手を肩書で呼ぶ習慣があることです。自分の会社の中だけではなく, ビジネス相手の会社の人も「社長」とか「部長」と呼びます。名前だけの名刺ですと相手の肩書がわかりません。しかし, 直接に聞くのはためらわれますし, また自分から肩書を名乗るのも不自然。ですから, お互いに, 名刺に会社名, そして肩書が書いてある名刺を交換し合うことが必要となるわけです。

Q Why are business cards necessary at work?

A Business cards are not unique to Japan. It is said that the origin of business cards dates back to China. When meeting a high government official, the person in the lower position would carve his name onto a piece of slivered bamboo to give to the official. The following reasons account for why attention is given to the fondness of the Japanese for business cards.

The first is that Japanese names are written in Kanji. Because many different characters have the same pronunciation, it is difficult to know just by its pronunciation what characters are actually used; hence, business cards serve as a convenient means to make clear how a person's name is written.

In the name NAGAI Hiroshi for instance, NAGAI can be written as 永井, 長井 or 長居 and Hiroshi can be written as 博, 浩, 宏 or 弘. There are many different character combinations that can be used for the same name that cannot be discerned by ear.

Another reason is the custom in Japanese society of calling a person by title not only in one's company but also for people in other companies. Businessmen from other companies are called by their titles such as *shachō* (president) or *buchō* (general manager). A name-only business card does not reveal position, and there is hesitancy in outright asking and an unnaturalness in declaring it on one's own initiative. This is why it is necessary to exchange business cards that state both the name of the company and position.

6

Puzzling Features of the Japanese School System

Question なぜ，日本の学校にはがんじがらめの規則が あるのですか?

Answer

　日本では，公立の小学校では制服もなく比較的自由な雰囲気ですが，中学校になると，がぜん規則が厳しくなります。

　中学校で特に規則が厳しくなる理由として，このくらいの年齢で子供たちは思春期に入り，親に対しても社会に対しても反抗的になる時期であることが背景にあります。

　ですから，厳しいルールを定めておかないと，この厄介な年齢の子供たちを制御することは難しい，と日本の学校の先生たちは考えているようです。一方，親も，家庭ではかなり甘い育て方をしておきながら，子供たちが手に負えなくなると，学校できちんとしたしつけをしてほしいと期待します。行動や身だしなみについて細かな規則を学校が作ることも，それが子供の人格や感情を損なうものだとは考えていません。

　難しい年頃だからこそ，個々人の自主性を尊重しようというアメリカの学校と，集団で規律を守らせることによって個人の責任を自覚させようとする日本との違いが，ここに大きく出ているようです。

　日本人は集団の中にいることに一種の安心感を持ちますので，その集団を平穏に維持するための規則に縛られることに対してあまり抵抗を感じないという傾向も，がんじがらめの規則を認めている理由の1つかも知れません。

Q Why are there so many constricting regulations in Japanese schools?

A Japanese public elementary schools are relatively liberal and uniforms are not required, but this takes a sudden turn in junior high school.

The reason why strict regulations are enforced especially in junior high school is that children of this age enter puberty, an age of rebellion against parents and society.

Japanese school teachers believe controlling students at this rebellious stage to be difficult if strict rules were not laid down. On the other hand, parents are too lenient and permissive with their children and look to the school to provide strict discipline when the children get out of hand. They do not feel that these rules made by the school covering every little detail from how students should act to their appearance, in any way, ignores the individuality and feelings of the students.

A great difference can be seen between the American school system of respecting independence especially at this difficult stage, and the Japanese school system of instilling awareness of individual responsibility by observing group rules.

The Japanese feel a sense of security belonging to a group and the fact that they do not resist being bound to the rules to maintain group harmony may be a reason behind why these restrictive regulations are adhered to.

Question なぜ，日本の学校はクラスの人数があんなに多いのですか？

Answer　　太平洋戦争後，平和が訪れ，日本の人口は急上昇します。1945年には約7200万人だった人口は，1950年には8320万人，1970年には1億を超え，たった25年間で3000万人も人口が増えてしまったのです。

　1947年に新しく教育基本法，学校教育法が制定され，教育の機会均等という理念のもとに，小学校，中学校は義務教育となり，すべての子供が学校に行くことになりました。そのために学校の数が足りなくなってしまったのです。

　従って，1960年代までの小学校では，1クラスに50人を超える生徒を収容せざるをえないという事態が続いたのです。その後，出生率の低下により，1980年ごろからは小学校の生徒数が減少し始めます。そして現在は，1クラスが40人を超えることはなくなりました。それでも，欧米の1クラスの人数に比べると多いのは事実です。

　高学歴化で多くの生徒が上に進み，教室の過密状態はそのまま，中学，高校，大学へと持ち込まれていきますが，その間，学校の新設は進みましたし，高校生の数のピークも1990年前後には減少しています。日本の教育過密もやっと落ち着いてきたと言えるようです。

Q Why are classes in Japanese elementary schools so large?

A Peace at the end of World War II resulted in a sharp rise in population. The population which stood at 72 million in 1945 rose to 83.2 million in 1950 and exceeded 100 million in 1970. The population increased by 30 million in a mere 25 years.

The Fundamental Law of Education and the School Education Law newly enacted in 1947 resulted in elementary and junior high schools becoming compulsory that enabled all children to receive an education under the philosophy of equal educational opportunities for all. As a result, there was a shortage of schools to accommodate all of the students.

Elementary school classes were forced to accommodate more than 50 students per class, and this situation continued until the 1960s. With the decline in birthrate, the number of pupils per class in elementary schools began to decline from around the 1980s. Now it does not exceed 40, but it still is a large number compared to the number of pupils per class in the United States.

With the importance placed on a high educational background, many students go on to pursue higher education and the overcrowded classroom situation continues on through junior high, high school and the university levels. However, the overcrowding in the Japanese classrooms has finally begun to ease with new schools that have come up in the meantime and the decline in the high school student population from around the 1990s.

Question　なぜ，日本では新学期が4月に始まるのですか？

Answer　日本の近代的な教育制度は，1872年（明治5年）の学制の発布からスタートします。学制はフランスの学校制度を参考にしており，4月を学年の始まりとしました。

　大正時代に一時，始業を9月にした学校もありましたが，日本の財政年度が4月から翌年3月までであることを考えると，いろいろな面で4月始業が便利なのです。

　4月は，日本では桜の咲く春の盛りですから，新しいスタートにふさわしい時期でもあり，制度としてごく自然に受け入れられていると言えるでしょう。季節感に敏感な日本人には，これから寒さに向かう秋の9月から始業というアメリカの制度のほうが不自然に思えます。

　しかし，学期の違いは，アメリカの学校に留学しようとする学生たちには少々迷惑です。どうしても空白の半年ができてしまい，日本の大学にもどっても1年留年をしなければならないことが多くなるのです。

　日本では，高校からストレートに有名大学に入ることが誇りとされますから（決してほめられたことではありませんが——），浪人して大学に入り，さらに留学すると，学期の始まりの違いで日本にもどってから卒業までにまた1年，2年余計にかかってしまうので困るのです。

Q Why does the new school year in Japan begin in April?

A The modern educational system in Japan began with the educational system promulgated in 1872 modeled after the French school system which began in April.

At one time during the Taisho period (1912–26), there were schools that began in September, but since the fiscal year in Japan begins in April and ends in March of the following year, it was deemed more convenient in many aspects to begin in April.

April is the height of spring when the cherry blossoms bloom and a most suitable time for a new start; hence, an April start was accepted as a matter of course. The Japanese are sensitive to the change in seasons and believe that the American system of beginning in September in the autumn with the cold of winter already on its way as unnatural.

Differences in the school-year system cause some inconvenience to students who wish to study abroad in the United States. A half year is wasted waiting to get in and oftentimes another year is wasted when coming back to the Japanese university because of having to repeat a year.

Entering a well-known university on the first try is considered something to be proud of (but certainly not something to be complimented on) and when a student fails to get in on the first try, another year has to be spent preparing for the entrance examination again. It is an inconvenience to have to spend an extra one or two years to graduate.

Question　なぜ，みんな塾に行くのですか？

Answer

　アメリカでも，ハーバード大学，プリンストン大学などのエリート大学の卒業証書が，社会で成功するためのパスポートだと言われているそうで，特に最近，エリート大学への進学率の高い高校における受験競争は厳しくなったと聞いています。

　そのために，家庭教師を雇ったり，パソコン通信やファックスなどによる通信添削を受けたり，また，高校が無料の補習コースを設けたりするそうですね。

　日本でも家庭教師に頼っていた時期がありますが，家庭教師では激化する受験戦争に対応できず，そこで大隆盛となったのが塾，そして予備校です。

　昔から予備校といったものは存在していました。しかし，旧制中学に高等学校の受験生のための補習科があった程度で，今日のような一大受験産業にまでなったのは，この何十年かのようです。

　日本の入学試験の多くは，機械的なペーパー・テストで受験生をふるい落とすものですから，その試験を突破するには，画一的な学校の授業の知識だけではむりで，特別の訓練が必要となります。そのために受験向けのテキスト，問題を次々と作って提供する力は，塾，予備校でない

Q Why do many students attend cram schools?

A In the United States, a diploma from one of the elite universities such as Harvard, Yale, Princeton, etc. is regarded as a passport to success in society. Recently, competition has become stiff to get into high schools having a large number of graduates successfully entering these elite universities.

Various methods are employed to ensure success such as: hiring private tutors, having papers corrected through computer networks and facsimiles, and high schools holding free supplementary courses.

There was a time in Japan too, when people relied on private tutors, but private tutors could not cope with the intensifying entrance examination competition, giving rise to the flourishing of cram schools and places offering after-school lessons.

Cram schools existed from before; however, they were limited to being supplementary courses for junior high school students under the prewar system to prepare them for their high school entrance examination. In only a matter of decades, cram schools grew into the greatest entrance examination industry seen today.

Japan's entrance examination weeds out applicants by a rote-learning type of written test. Special training is required to pass these tests. The standard education received at school alone is not enough to pass these difficult tests. This is where the cram schools come in to bring out the best of the students' ability through a series of texts containing

と持てません。

　もともと頭がいい学生ならともかく, 今一息という人には, 塾での特訓がモノを言いますから, 多くの学生が塾に通います。小学生の40%, 中学生の50%, 高校生の60%が, 塾, 予備校に通っていると言われています。

questions prepared by the cram schools that are geared to pass the difficult entrance examination.

With the exception of people who are naturally bright, the intensive lessons offered at cram schools for those who need just a little extra push bring good results drawing many students to these cram schools. It is said that 40% of elementary school students, 50% of junior high school students and 60% of high school students attend some kind of after-school lessons and/or cram schools.

Question なぜ，大学にはあんなにたくさんのクラブが あるのですか?

Answer

　日本では，厳しい受験競争をくぐり抜けて大学にもぐりこんだら，後は就職活動に備えるだけというのが一般的です。

　学問を志して入学したわけでもなく，また自分の志望通りの学部に入ったわけでもない人も多いのですから，どうしてものんびりムードが漂います。

　必然，仲間を集めて，好きな活動に熱中することになります。特に高度成長期では卒業後の就職も心配なく，大学は一種のレジャーランドと化していったのです。

　クラブの活動の内容は学生の自主性に任せられていますので，長い歴史のあるクラブ以外に，ありとあらゆる同好会といったものが乱立しているのが，日本の大学の現状です。どこかの大学では「野宿研究会」「アイドル研究会」なるものまで登場しているそうです。

　アメリカの大学は，入学は比較的簡単だが，いざ入ると厳しい勉強が待っているし，学費は親からもらわず自分たちでまかなうというのが普通で，必然，アルバイトにも精を出さなければならないので，クラブ活動にうつつを抜かしている時間がない，と聞きました。学費や生活費は親からもらった上に，アルバイトで得た金はクラブ活動や遊びに使うという日本の学生とは，だいぶん違うようですね。

Q What accounts for the proliferation of clubs at Japanese universities?

A When a student finally manages to pass the stiff entrance examination and gets accepted to a university, usually the only thing left to do is to prepare for job hunting.

Students tend to be easy-going due to the fact that many did not enter universities with the intent to aspire for higher learning, nor did they enter the department of their choice.

Friends group together and become absorbed in a common activity they enjoy doing together. Especially in the period of high economic growth when there were no worries about employment after graduating, universities became recreational centers.

Club activities are left entirely up to the students and excluding clubs with a long history, there now exists all sorts of every conceivable kind of club. There is even a Sleeping-in-the-Open Nature Study Club and a Pop Idol Study Club at a certain university.

It is relatively easy to get accepted to American universities but once admitted, the students are required to buckle down in order to keep up with classes. Also, many American students are on their own once they enter university and must put in a lot of hours at work to earn their own tuition leaving no time to be involved in clubs. This differs greatly from Japanese students whose parents pay for their tuition and living expenses. What Japanese students earn at their part-time job go for club activities and other incidentals to spend as they please.

Question なぜ，大学では勉強しなくても卒業できるのですか？

Answer

　確かに日本の大学は，入るのは簡単，卒業するのは困難というアメリカの大学に比べて，入るのは困難，卒業するのは簡単です。

　もちろん日本の大学だって，専門の学問，技術を身につける所です。相当の努力をしなければ卒業できない学校はたくさんあります。それでも多くの日本の大学生が遊んでいるように見えるのは，講座が教師の一方的な講義で行われることが多いからではないでしょうか。

　学生は授業に出なくても，誰かのノートを借りるか，その講義の内容が書かれた本を読んでいれば，なんとか単位を取れるのです。

　また日本の大学では，何年も研究論文を書かなくても教師をしていられることが問題になったことがあります。大学教師のレベルの低さが，勉強をしない学生を生んでいるという人もいます。学生が教師を評価するシステムがあるというアメリカの大学の真剣さが，日本の大学にないことは事実です。

　それに，日本の大学の経営は，授業料の他に入ってくる毎年の莫大な受験料や入学金で賄われますから，新入生がドル箱です。そのためにも，とにかく勉強をしない学生でも，順に卒業してもらわなければ困るシステムになっている——といったら言い過ぎでしょうか。

Q Why is it possible to graduate from Japanese universities without studying?

A Compared to American universities where entering is easy and graduating is difficult, at Japanese universities entering is difficult and graduating is easy.

Of course, there are many Japanese universities where the students are required to study before they can be granted a diploma. But a great number of university students seem to be laid-back, perhaps stemming from the fact that the lectures are oftentimes carried out on a one-way basis on the part of the teacher.

Skipping classes is no problem. The student can always manage to receive credits for the courses by borrowing someone's notes or reading a book that covers the lectures.

It became an issue at Japanese universities that teachers who did not produce a paper for a number of years were allowed to remain on the faculty. There are people who say that the low level of the teachers at universities gives rise to students who do not study. The seriousness of the American university system where teachers are rated by the students does not exist in Japan.

The expense of running a Japanese university is covered by tuition as well as the exorbitant amount coming in from both the entrance examination and admission fees every year. The new student is a veritable cash box. It certainly is no exaggeration to say that the system would not function unless even students who do not study are permitted to graduate when their time comes.

Question なぜ，日本の英語教育は成果があがらないのですか？

Answer

　日本では，中学1年から英語教育が始まり，少なくとも高校3年までは続けるのが普通です。しかし，なぜか話せない，聞けないという人ばかり！　その原因は，過去の日本の英語教育はreading, writingに重点が置かれていたからです。明治以来，欧米文化に追いつくために，英語の文献から知識を読み取ることが第一だったのです。

　太平洋戦争の後，英語教育が盛んになりますが，どうしても，reading中心の教育を受けた教師が教えるのですから，hearing, speakingの訓練の環境ができていませんでした。

　現在では，語学のラボの設置や，外国人教師などの採用によってpracticalな英語を学習する環境が整ってきましたので，これから変わってくることは間違いありません。

　しかし1つ問題があります。文部省の指導要領というものです。指導要領によれば，中学3年の間に学習する単語は約1000語と制限されており，また，文章の構造についても，学年ごとに段階が決められたりしていて，言葉を学ぶ上では何とも不自由なのです。

　教科書は文部省の検定を受けなければなりませんので，どうしても画一的な教科書ばかりとなり，英語教育を窮屈にしてしまっているようです。

Q Why can't the way English is taught in Japan produce people who can use English?

A Schools in Japan start teaching English from the first year of junior high school continuing at least until the third year of high school, but the students are unable to speak or to comprehend English! The reason lies in the fact that in the past, Japan relied heavily on the reading and writing method of teaching English. During the Meiji period (1868–1912) onward, utmost priority was placed on reading works written in English for the purpose of acquiring knowledge in order to catch up with the West.

Learning English became popular after World War II, but English was taught by teachers who were trained under the method that emphasized reading. There were no qualified teachers to teach hearing and speaking.

The situation is sure to change for the better with emphasis now being placed on practical language learning by the installation of language laboratories and the hiring of foreign language teachers.

However, a problem lies with the Ministry of Education's guidelines. The guideline limits the English vocabulary that is to be learned during the three years of junior high school to about 1,000. Even the type of sentence structure that can be taken up in each grade level is stipulated, which greatly hampers language learning.

Textbooks must first undergo a screening by the Ministry of Education resulting for the most part in standardized textbooks making English language learning too confining.

Question なぜ，筆で書くことはないのに，学校に書道の時間があるのですか？

Answer

　今の世の中，祝儀袋，不祝儀袋に上書きをしたり，結婚式などの受付の名簿に筆で書かされることがあるくらいで，それまでも最近はサイン・ペンで書くことが多くなりましたから，日常で私たちが筆で文字を書くことは，めったにない，と言っていいと思います。

　しかし「書」は古来，日本人の教養の1つとして欠かせないものでした。「書道」という言葉になっているように，単に文字を書く技術のことではなく，文字を書くことが1つの精神修養になっているのです。

　筆で文字を書くことを習いはじめたときは，一画，一画をていねいに書いていきます。同じ一本の線を引くときも，それぞれ正しい書き方があるわけです。

　その正しい筆順を知っていないと筆で書くことができないことから，漢字やひらがなの書き方の基本を身につけるために欠かせない手段となっています。現在でも，小学校，中学校で授業の1つとされているのはそのためです。

　墨の色の濃淡や，それぞれの筆の使い方によって，個性が出てきますし，美的な鑑賞の対象にもなっているのが書道です。

Q Why is calligraphy taught in schools using a brush when people no longer write with brushes anymore?

A The Japanese rarely write with a brush nowadays except when addressing congratulatory envelopes, condolence envelopes and listing their name to the register at wedding receptions. And now that more people have started using felt pens, very seldom does the opportunity arise to use a brush in everyday life.

From long ago, calligraphy was an essential part of the cultural training of the Japanese. As the term *shodō* (calligraphy) indicates, it is not merely the skill and technique of writing characters that are emphasized, but an emphasis on writing characters as a way to provide mental and moral training for the mind.

When calligraphy is first learned, the strokes are written carefully and deliberately one stroke at a time. There are even different ways of making a straight line depending on the character.

Writing with a brush requires knowing the proper stroke order, and calligraphy is an indispensable means of acquiring the basics of writing Kanji and *hiragana* (a cursive form of writing commonly used for writing native words). This is why calligraphy is one of the subjects taught in elementary and junior high schools.

One's individuality shows by how the brush is used and by the light and dark shadings of the India ink seen in the finished work. Calligraphy is appreciated as a form of art.

Question なぜ，日本人は卒業式で泣くことがあるのですか？

Answer

　　日本人は集団の中にいないと安心できないという性向があるようで，よく「ウチの会社は──」とか，「ウチの学校は──」と言います。

　「ウチ」というのは「〜の中」という意味ですが，この場合は「われわれ」「自分」のという意味になります。会社で出世しなくても，また，いじめっこがいる学校でも，その属している集団はみんな「ウチの」ものなのです。

　　そういう状況の中では，集団の他のメンバーが嫌がることはしないように自制しますし，他のメンバーが喜ぶことをするし，他のメンバーとうまくやっていくようにします。そこに仲間意識が生まれます。

　　卒業式はそういう仲間との別れです。集団の解体です。個々に親しくなった人とはこれからも友人として続いていくでしょうが，集団の解体は避けられません。そこに，ある感傷が生まれます。それが「蛍の光」や武田鉄矢（海援隊）の「贈る言葉」などの歌で増幅されてムードが高まったときに，涙が生まれるのです。

　　卒業式の意味の英語はcommencement。原義は「始まること；開始」ということで，まさにここから「人生」が始まるわけですから，未来に対する緊張感や希望で一杯で，「泣く」理由もないわけです。卒業式の受け止め方に，日本と根本的な違いがありますね。

Q Why do the Japanese sometimes cry at graduation?

A The Japanese do not feel secure being out of a group. They refer to their company as *uchi no kaisha* (our company) or to their school as *uchi no gakkō* (our school).

Uchi means "being a part of" or "our/my" in this case. One would still call one's affiliated group as *uchi* or "our" even if one is not promoted at all in the company or even if there are bullies at school.

As a member of the group, the Japanese try to get along with the other members by showing restraint in not doing anything that would displease, but rather, by doing things that would please the other members in the group. A sense of camaraderie develops as a result.

Graduation is a time to part from one's fellow classmates, in other words, a dismantling of the group. Although the friendship of close friends formed within the group would still continue in the future, the dismantling of the group cannot be avoided. A certain sentiment prevails that is intensified by the song, "Auld Lang Syne" and TAKEDA Tetsuya's (with the Kaientai Band) "A Message for You." The mood builds up to a height and is released in tears.

A graduation ceremony is called commencement in English and its original meaning is, "to begin." Embarking on a new life is filled with hope and anxiety for what the future may hold. There is no reason to cry about it. There are basic differences in the way Americans and Japanese view graduation.

Question なぜ，大学生は親に学費を出してもらうのですか？

Answer

　　日本の大学は，アメリカの大学のように勉強をしたいという人に広く門を開けているわけではありません。

　　日本では大学に入るためには，小学校，中学校，高等学校，そして大学と，次々に受験戦争に勝ち抜いて来なければなりません。

　　ところが，往々にして，大学受験に失敗して浪人することもあります。しかも，2年も3年も浪人を続ける人もいますが，だからといって希望の大学に入れるわけでもなく，高校を出たらできるだけ早く大学に入らないと，ますます道は厳しくなるばかりです。日本では，アメリカの大学のように，大学の学費を自分でためてから——などと悠長なことを言っているひまはないのです。

　　また，なんと言っても学歴社会ですから，子供の出世を期待する親は，アルバイトをする時間があるくらいなら勉強をしろ，アルバイトで稼ぐくらいの金は出してやる，それよりも少しでも早く，少しでもいい大学に入るように——と考えるのです。親は子供の教育を投資と考えているようでもあります。

Q Why do Japanese students let their parents pay for all of their college expenses?

A Japanese universities are unlike American universities where the doors are opened wide for people who truly want to study.

In order to enter a university in Japan, one has to survive a series of stiff examinations taken in elementary school, junior high school, high school, and university.

Students often fail the university entrance examination and have to study to take them again. There are those who give it a second or third try, but this does not guarantee them admittance to the university of their choice. Students have to try to enter a university in the least possible time after graduating from high school, otherwise passing the test will become more and more difficult. Unlike American students who save to pay for their tuition, Japanese students have no time to be thinking about the other aspects except to pass.

Japan is a society that places great importance on educational background. Japanese parents have high expectations on the success of their children and would much rather see their children study than work in their free time. They regard paying for their children's expenses and having them enter a better university in as short a time as possible to be more practical than to have their children work to earn whatever they can at their part-time job. They consider their children's education to be an investment.

7

日本の
結婚式・葬式の
ふしぎ

Puzzling Features of
Weddings and Funerals
in Japan

Question なぜ，結婚式は教会や神社で，葬式はお寺で，などということができるのですか？

Answer そもそも日本では，結婚式は宗教的儀式ではありませんでした。昔は，花婿の家で作法に基づいて行われていたもので，神社や教会で行うようになったのは，明治以降になってからのことです。特に，今一般的に行われている神前結婚式は，大正天皇の結婚式をまねて流行し，一般に定着したと言われています。

神社はある土地の守り神でもあり，そこに住む者としてはその神社で結婚の誓いの式を挙げることは理にかなっています。教会も地域に根ざしたもので，キリスト教の信者であれば，教会で結婚式を挙げるのは当然のことです。

しかし，そもそも宗教的なものに縛られていなかったのですから，だんだん形式的になり，教会であれ，お好みで式が挙げられるようになってしまいました。

葬式の場合は結婚式とは少し違います。仏教の各派は長い歴史を経て日本の社会に溶け込んでいて，今でも，寺は多くの家の菩提寺となっているからです。必然的に葬式は仏式で行われることがほとんどになります。

現代は核家族の時代ですから，先祖代々の墓には戻らず，それぞれが自分の家の墓を持つことも多いのですが，その場合でも，葬儀は家の宗派に合わせて行うことが普通です。

Q Why are weddings held at churches or shrines and funerals at temples?

A The wedding ceremony in Japan was traditionally not a religious ceremony. In the old days, they were held at the bridegroom's house based on the decorums of etiquette. It was not until the Meiji period (1868–1912) onward that wedding ceremonies came to be held at shrines and churches. It is said that *Shintō* weddings, which are widely prevalent today, came into vogue after the wedding of Emperor Taishō and became firmly established with the general public.

The shrine is the guardian deity of a particular locality, and it stands within reason for the residents living in the region to hold wedding ceremonies at the shrine. Churches also have deep roots in a particular locality and many Christians hold wedding ceremonies at the church.

Since wedding ceremonies in Japan are not traditionally bound by religion, where to hold the ceremony has become but a mere formality based on a matter of preference whether held at a church or elsewhere.

Funerals differ somewhat from weddings. The various Buddhist sects have had a long history before becoming a part of Japanese society. The temple serves as a family temple for many households even today and the reason why funerals are conducted according to Buddhist rites.

In the present age of the nuclear family, many households have their own grave plots and do not intend to be buried in their ancestral grave, but even then, funerals are still conducted according to the family's traditional religious sect.

Question　なぜ，結婚式を挙げてはいけない日がある のですか？

Answer　　日本の暦には，毎年，いい日，悪い日，普通の日 が決まっています。それは六曜と言われる，そも そも星占いからきた俗信によるもので，次の内 容になっています。

　　　先勝──午前の運はいいが，午後は悪くなる 日。
　　　友引──朝晩はいいが，昼は悪い日。文字に友 を引っ張る，という意味があるので，こ の日には葬式を避ける。

　　　先負──午前の運は悪く，午後はいい日。

　　　仏滅──すべてが悪い日。
　　　大安──一日中，運がいい日。
　　　赤口──正午のみ運がいい日。

　　これを見るとおわかりの通り，仏滅という日 が最悪とされていますから，この日には結婚式 を避けるのが普通です。最近の若い人の間には， このような俗信を気にしない人も増えました が，当人たちはともかく，親や親戚の中には嫌が る人がいますから，この仏滅の日におめでたい ことを強行する人は少ないようです。

　　ある結婚式場の話によると，仏滅の日の結婚 式は，大安の日の3分の1程度ということで，サー ビス料金を設定して，仏滅の日の挙式をすすめ ているところもあります。

Q Why are weddings not held on certain days?

A There are good, bad, and ordinary days designated in the Japanese calendar every year. This folk belief, called *Rokuyō,* or the six basic labels printed on a traditional Japanese calendar indicating how auspicious a given day is, was derived from astrology. The six labels are:

Senshō—a day lucky in the morning but unlucky in the afternoon.

Tomobiki—a day lucky in the morning and night but unlucky at noontime. As indicated by the characters, it carries a meaning of pulling a friend along and it is therefore avoided in the scheduling of funerals.

Senbu—a day unlucky in the morning but lucky in the afternoon.

Butsumetsu—a day unlucky all day.

Taian—a day lucky all day.

Shakkou—a day only lucky at noontime.

As seen from the above, *butsumetsu* is regarded as a most unlucky day and most people avoid scheduling weddings on this day. More and more young people nowadays are not bothered by these superstitions, but because there are many parents and relatives who do, there are not too many people who go ahead and hold auspicious events on *butsumetsu.*

Because the number of weddings held on *butsumetsu* is about one-third of that held on *taian*, a certain wedding hall reduces its rate for ceremonies held on *butsumetsu* to encourage more people to get married on this day.

Question　なぜ，日本人は葬儀や結婚式に，そろって黒い服を着るのですか?

Answer

　洋の東西を問わず，黒というのは厳粛な感じを作り出す色です。従って，葬儀のような悲しみに包まれた儀式の席には，黒，あるいは黒っぽい色の服を着るのが適当であるとされてきました。

　黒は不吉さも表しますから，そもそもは身内の死を迎えた遺族が着るのが当然とされていましたが，今では遺族に限らず，多くの人が黒い服で焼香に来ます。

　その黒服を日本では結婚式にも着るのが，外国人には不思議に見えるのでしょう。しかも女性は訪問着やら，しゃれたドレスで来るのに，男性はなぜか黒，またはダーク・スーツです。

　その理由としては，1つには，日本の朝廷に仕える貴族で，位が高い者は黒の衣冠束帯に身を包んだことがあります。また，改まって席に出るときの武士が黒い着物を着たこともあります。

　それに，明治になってあっという間に日本に入ってきた，様々な欧米のファッションの中の，黒のフロック・コートや燕尾服，黒のモーニング，黒のシルク・ハット——厳粛を重んじた英国のビクトリア朝のこのファッションが，日本では「式服」という形になり，結婚式でも葬式でも，ネクタイを換えるだけで兼用できるようになったということです。

Q Why do the Japanese all wear black to funerals and weddings?

A Whether in the East or West, black brings out a mood of solemnness and austerity. At funerals, a ceremony enveloped in sorrow, wearing black or nearly black is considered most appropriate.

Black represents ill-omen and bereaving family members traditionally wore black. Now, black is worn not only by the bereaving family members but also by people who come to pay their respects.

Wearing black at weddings in Japan may strike non-Japanese as odd. Moreover, while women wear a semi-ceremonial kimono or a stylish dress, men are clad in a black or a dark suit.

One of the reasons is that the nobility of high ranking who served in the Imperial Court wore a black traditional court dress. Also, the samurai wore a black kimono on formal occasions.

In the Meiji period (1868–1912), many kinds of Western fashions found their way into Japan and among them were the black frock coats, black swallow-tailed coats, black morning coats, black silk hats—all fashions from the English court of Queen Victoria that placed importance on solemnness. These became formal wear in Japan that could be worn to both weddings and funerals by substituting a different necktie.

Question なぜ，結婚披露宴にあんなにたくさんのスピーチが必要なのですか？

Answer

　アメリカ映画で，結婚をしてから後で，相手を親に紹介するというシーンがよくありますが，日本もかなりアメリカ的になったとはいえ，そんなことを子供にされたら，日本の親は肝をつぶしてしまうでしょう。婚姻は当人たちの合意で成立するものとはいえ，日本ではまだ，家と家との結びつきという考え方も強く残っているからです。

　そこで結婚披露宴では，婚姻によって新しく生じる人間関係を円滑にするために，親戚，上司，先輩，友人たちを，次々とスピーチの席に駆り立てていくわけです。

　その中には，ほとんど関係はないのに，相手の家に対するデモンストレーションのために有名人に出席してもらったり，またその人が退屈で通りいっぺんの挨拶をしたりで，ますますくだらない披露宴になっていくことがあります。とにかくスピーチの数が多すぎることは，私たち日本人でさえ認めざるをえないことです。

　しかし，次第に親も子供も家という観念が薄くなってきた世代に入り，最近，型通りの披露宴を嫌って独自の演出をすることも多くなりましたから，つまらないスピーチを聞かされることも少なくなっていくと思います。

Q Why are so many speeches made at wedding receptions?

A There are scenes in American movies where the parents of a just-married couple are introduced to their child's spouse for the very first time. Although the Japanese have become very much Americanized, Japanese parents would be shocked if their child were to pull off something like that on them. Marriage is basically an agreement reached between two people, but the idea that marriage is a forging of ties between two families is still firmly entrenched in Japan.

Relatives, superiors, seniors and friends all make speeches one after another at wedding receptions in order that the new human relationships formed through marriage will proceed harmoniously.

There are families that invite well-known people to whom they have even the remotest connection with to display their standing to the other family. At times the wedding is transformed into a frivolous show by the boring and perfunctory speeches given by well-known people. Even the Japanese themselves admit that there are entirely too many speeches made at wedding receptions.

Both parents and children alike in the new generation have increasingly come to view the family as a remote concept. Many people are fed up with formal ceremonies and are opting to have a wedding catered to their personal taste, and with it the chances of having to bear with boring speeches will certainly lessen.

Ｑuestion　なぜ，こんなに結婚式の費用が高いのですか？

Ａnswer

　日本ではまだ，結婚式を家と家との結びつきで考える人がたくさんいますから，相手の家のことを考えると，あまり結婚式の費用にケチなことは言えないという心理があります。

　そもそも日本では，昔から結婚式には金がかかるものだと言われています。「一生の極彩色は嫁入りの日」（誹風柳多留拾遺）と川柳にもあるように，女性にとっては嫁入りが一生の中の最大の出来事です。

　戦後，昔のように結婚式を花婿の家で行うということはほとんどなくなり，ホテルや結婚式場を利用しますので，ますますお金がかかるようになりました。結婚式場も様々な趣向をこらした披露宴を宣伝したり，花嫁は2度も3度も衣装を替えたり，次第に派手な結婚式になっていきました。しかし，1960年から80年代にかけては，日本は著しい経済成長期で，国民所得も大きく増えましたので，海外旅行なども含めて，日本人がちょっとぜいたくができた時代でもあったのです。1995年の調査で，一般庶民の結婚式の費用の平均でも，335万円ぐらいになっています。

　しかし，ある銀行の調査で，結婚後のカップルの3割が，結婚式にお金を掛け過ぎたと後悔しており，1990年代に入ってからは，少しずつ，不必要なお金をかけないで，若い人なりのアイディアで演出した結婚式が増えつつあるそうです。

Q Why does it cost so much to hold a wedding?

A There are many Japanese who regard marriage as an alliance between two families and they feel that they cannot be too stingy about the cost of the wedding to make an impression on the other family.

From long ago it was said in Japan that holding a wedding required spending much money. According to the *Haifū-yanagidaru-shūi*, a book of *senryū* (a comic *haiku* poem), a woman's wedding day is a once-in-a-lifetime day when she is most brilliantly colored.

The time-honored practice of holding the wedding ceremony at the bridegroom's house was very rarely carried out after the war. Hotels and weddings halls were utilized instead which resulted in having to spend more money. Weddings became more and more gaudy as wedding halls took to advertising their selection of a variety of elaborate receptions as well as having the bride change to a different outfit two or three times during the reception. The 1960s to the 1980s was a period of high economic growth which saw a rise in the national income that enabled the Japanese to become a little extravagant and to take overseas trips. According to a 1995 survey, the average amount spent for holding a wedding came out to be about 3.35 million yen (US $30,000).

However, according to a bank survey, 30% of couples after their wedding regretted spending too much on their wedding. The 1990s marked a trend where more and more young people are opting for an original wedding that does not require spending money unnecessarily.

Question なぜ，日本人は団体旅行でハネムーンに行く人が多いのですか？

Answer

　大きな理由は，団体旅行では費用がぐんと経済的だからです。2人だけの特別のツアーを旅行代理店に組んでもらうと，団体旅行の一員で行くときの1.5倍ぐらいかかります。

　費用を全部，親が出してくれるというのならともかく，自分たちで負担しようとなると，結婚式の費用に旅行の費用の両方は，若い人たちには苦しい金額です。

　せっかくのハネムーンですから，ずっと2人きりでいたいだろうに，と勘ぐる必要もありません。最近のカップルは結婚前に，十分に2人っきりの時間を持っていますから，新婚旅行というよりも，初めての土地，見知らぬ国への観光旅行を楽しむという雰囲気のほうが強いようです。

　それに外国に行った場合，語学に不安がある日本人ですから，特に男としては，せっかくの楽しい旅行なのに，相手をちゃんとエスコートできないなどということになったらという心配があります。しかも，物騒だと言われる海外旅行で，とんでもない目に会うことも心配です。

　となると，一応は安心して行動を任せられる添乗員付きの団体旅行に加わるほうが，はるかに安心できるというわけです。

Q Why do many Japanese couples go on a honeymoon with a tour group?

A This is largely due to the fact that joining a tour group is most economical. The price of having a travel agent arrange a tour just for two would come out to be 1.5 times more than what a tour would cost.

This would not be a problem if the parents agree to foot the entire trip, but it would be a problem if the young couple were obligated to bear the entire cost of the trip as well as the cost of the wedding.

There is no need to feel that the couple would want to be by themselves on their honeymoon. Couples of today have had ample time to be by themselves before marriage. They are far more impressed at setting foot in another land and going sightseeing in a new locality than the fact that they are on their honeymoon.

Also, the Japanese are insecure about their linguistic ability when going abroad. Men especially, worry about not being able to properly escort their partner on what is to be a trip they had been looking forward to with pleasure. They also worry about encountering the unexpected in overseas travel like the dangers they had been warned about.

They feel far safer joining a tour group and leaving matters entirely in the hands of the capable tour conductor.

Question　なぜ，お寺で結婚式が行われないのですか?

Answer

　　　ないわけではありませんが，お寺で結婚式が行われるのは，日本で行われる全結婚式の約2%だそうです。

　　寺というと，現代では葬儀を行うところというイメージが先に立ちますから，めでたい結婚式を寺で行うことには，どうしても抵抗を感じる人が多いのです。

　　本来は寺というのは，亡くなった人のためにだけあったのではなく，そこで僧が修行をし，また，地域社会に根ざして，庶民も日常の生活の中で仏の教えに接する場でありました。

　　しかし現代では，信仰の場として寺を訪ねる人は少なく，多くの人は，観光の名所か，あるいは単に，死者の霊をとむらう場所としてしか認識しなくなってしまいました。

　　「ホトケ(仏)」は仏陀，仏像というのが第一の意味ですが，転じて「死者；死者の霊」の意味で使いますし，家にある仏壇は亡くなった人の位牌を祀るところです。やはり，あまりにも寺や仏教は死者との結びつきが強くなりすぎたようです。

　　禅宗の寺は，座禅などで精神修養をする場として，若い人の間にもそれなりの人気を持っていますが，そうは言っても，禅寺でも結婚式を挙げる人はほとんどありません。

Q Why aren't weddings held at temples?

A There are some weddings that are held at temples. Of all the weddings in Japan, roughly 2% are held at temples.

However, the image of temples as a place for holding funerals first comes to mind and many Japanese are not receptive to the idea of holding auspicious events like weddings at temples.

Originally, temples served not only to officiate at death but also as a place where Buddhist priests trained. Temples have also taken root in the community and have served in the daily lives of the common people by being a place where they could come into contact with Buddhism.

There are few people nowadays who use temples as a place of worship. Many people regard temples as a place to visit for their historic significance or because they see temples as simply a place to pray for the repose of the dead.

The foremost meaning of *hotoke* (Buddha) is the "Buddha" or "Buddhist image," but it also takes on the meaning of "a deceased person" or "a deceased person's spirit." The household altar in homes is where the memorial tablet of the deceased is enshrined. Temples and Buddhism seem to have too strong a connection to the dead.

A Zen temple is a place to undergo spiritual training through *zazen* (zen meditation). Zen has a following even among people in the younger generation, but even then, very few people would choose to hold a wedding ceremony at a Zen temple.

Question　なぜ，神社で葬式が行われないのですか？

Answer　神社は様々な神を祀ったところですが，神社の境内の中は神聖な場所であり，死を汚れ（けが）たものとして嫌っています。仏教とはまったく対照的です。

古事記や日本書紀に書かれた神話の中に，イザナギノミコトが亡くなった奥さんを「黄泉（よみ）の国」に行って連れ戻そうとするのですが，蛆（うじ）がわいたおぞましい妻の姿を見て，命からがら逃げ帰るという話があります。ミコトはなんとか逃げ帰るとさっそく体を清めて，「ああ，助かった」と安堵したのだそうです。

つまり神様でさえ死後の世界はまっぴらごめんというわけで，その神様を祀る神社に，死者が入ることを許さないのです。

神式で葬儀が行われる場合には，神棚や神殿はとびらを閉じ，白い紙で封をしてから行われます。つまり神様が見ている前では行わないのです。

現在，天皇家では神道に基づいて葬儀を行うことになっていますが，これは明治になって，神道が国家の保護を受けてきたことの名残で，江戸時代までは天皇家といえども，仏教で葬られていました。

Q Why aren't funerals held at shrines?

A In Shintoism, shrines are where the myriads of gods and goddesses are enshrined and death was despised because death was thought to defile the sacred precincts of the shrine. This is in sharp contrast to Buddhism.

According to the mythologies recorded in the *Kojiki* (712 Records of Ancient Matters) and the *Nihonshoki* (720 Chronicles of Japan), Izanagi no Mikoto, a deity, pursues his wife to the nether world (Yomi no Kuni) after her death in an attempt to bring her back, but he finds her horribly transformed and infested with maggots. Izanagi flees and barely escapes with his life. After his return, he purifies himself at once by bathing. He then says with relief, "I'm safe!"

In other words, even the deities did not want anything to do with death; hence, a deceased person was denied entry to shrines that enshrined these deities.

Before a funeral could be conducted at a shrine, the doors of the altar and sanctuary had to be first closed and covered with white paper. It was not conducted where it could be seen by the deities.

Presently, the Imperial family conducts funerals based on Shintoism as a vestige of the custom that was practiced when Shintoism was declared the state religion in the Meiji period (1868–1912). However, until the Edo period (1600–1868), even the Imperial family was buried in accordance with Buddhist rites.

Question なぜ，葬儀の後，法事が何度も行われるのですか？

Answer

インド起源の法事の日，中国のしきたりに基づく日，日本古来の祖先崇拝の日と，それぞれ起源の違う死者の弔いの行事が重なりあって，今の日本の法事になっています。

本来，仏教の行事としては，亡くなった日から17〜47日の供養しかありませんでした。中国のしきたりでは，百ヵ日，一周忌，三周忌があり，さらに七周忌，十三周忌，二十三周忌，三十三周忌，五十周忌，百周忌，永代供養は日本独特のものです。

なぜ，日本にそんなにたくさんの法事があるかと言えば，日本古来の宗教である神道が祖先崇拝の宗教であり，日本人が祖先を祀ることにかけては，世界のどんな国の人よりも熱心であることが理由として挙げられると思います。

正月は今では新年を祝う行事となっていますが，そもそもは暮れから正月にかけて先祖の霊を供養する行事でした。お盆は今でも，日本の全国で守られている先祖の供養の行事です。そして，春，夏のお彼岸には，日本人は墓参りを欠かしません。家には仏壇を置いて先祖の霊を祀り，毎日，お供えをしている家もまだあります。

Q Why are memorial services held a number of times after a funeral?

A The Japanese memorial service of today is based on a combination of various origins of memorial services for the deceased derived from the memorial service tradition in India, conventions based on Chinese traditions, and ancestor worship in ancient Japan.

It was primarily a Buddhist memorial service conducted from the 17th day and lasting until the 47th day after death. Chinese convention prescribes these memorial services to be held 100 days, 1 year and 3 years after death (by Japanese reckoning that includes the year of death). But extending these services to 7 years, 13 years, 23 years, 33 years, 50 years, 100 years and in perpetuity after death is uniquely Japanese.

The reason why so many memorial services are held in Japan is because of Shintoism which is based on ancestor worship. The Japanese feel that they are second to none when it comes to dedication as far as ancestor worship is concerned.

New Year is now an event to celebrate the incoming year, but originally the period from the end of the year to New Year served as a time for holding a memorial service for the spirits of one's ancestors. Even today, the tradition of *obon* (the Buddhist festival of the dead) is followed throughout Japan. The Japanese also visit their family grave during the spring and summer equinox. Homes in Japan have a family altar dedicated to the ancestors and there are still homes where offerings are made every day.

Question　なぜ，お坊さんが結婚できるのですか？

Answer

　　キリスト教のカトリックとプロテスタントの違いに当てはめてみると，わかりやすいでしょう。

　　この場合，カトリックが仏教の天台宗や真言宗などの古代以来の仏教に相当し，プロテスタントが浄土真宗以後の民衆仏教に相当すると思ってください。

　　カトリックでは神父は妻帯は禁じられており，一方，プロテスタントの牧師は結婚ができます。日本の宗教の中では，カトリックにあたる天台宗や真言宗，また禅宗では僧侶の結婚を禁じているのに対して，一応，プロテスタントにあたる浄土真宗では結婚を認めているのです。

　　12世紀末に浄土真宗を起こした親鸞は，仏教者として初めて妻帯を実践した人です。親鸞は，世俗を捨てないで，庶民と同じような生活をしながら仏に身を捧げることができないといけないと悟りました。そこで，30歳で結婚し，家庭を持ちながら修行を続ける聖職者としての一生を送りました。

　　しかし，インド，スリランカ，タイなどに広まっている，修行によって個人の解脱をはかろうとする小乗仏教では，妻帯などは考えられないことです。

Q Why can priests marry?

A This would be easier to explain if the differences between Catholicism and Protestantism in Christianity were compared.

Think of Catholicism as the Tendai or Shingon sects of Buddhism existing from ancient times, and Protestantism as Buddhism for the masses from the Jodo Shin (True Pure Land) sect and other sects thereafter.

While Catholic priests are prohibited from marrying, Protestant clergy are allowed to marry. Priests in the Tendai and Shingon sects as well as Zen which all fall under the Catholic category, are prohibited from marrying. Priests in the Jodo Shin sect, which falls under the Protestant category are allowed to marry.

Shinran, the founder of Jodo Shin sect at the end of the twelfth century, was the first Buddhist priest to marry. He felt that one had to serve Buddha by not abandoning the secular world and by living the same kind of life as the common people. Shinran married at age thirty and lived out his life as a priest who continued his training while supporting a family.

Theravadin Buddhism strives for individual deliverance from earthly bondage through training. Theravadin Buddhism which spread throughout the Southeast Asian countries such as India, Sri Lanka and Thailand does not permit priests to marry.

Question なぜ，日本人はまだ若いのにお見合いをするのですか？

Answer

　1987年の厚生省の調査では，恋愛結婚の比率は74％であるのに対し，お見合いは24％でした。ところが，1992年の調査では，この数字は78％と15％になっています。

　外国の人の日本人に対する先入観の中に，日本人はお見合いをするものだという意識が強いようですが，上の数字のように，実際には見合いをする人は，かなり少なくなっています。とは言っても，日本の若い女性たちが見合いを否定しているかというと，そうでもありませんが――。

　未婚の女性たちが期待する結婚相手の条件は「三高」，つまり「高学歴」「高収入」「高い身長」の3つだそうで，この条件の人を自分の周囲にいる手近な恋愛の相手の中から見つけようとするのは至難のことです。となるとお見合いが有力な相手探しの方法であることは，今も変わりません。

　お見合いは，そもそも江戸時代に庶民の間に生まれた習慣ですが，昔は男性社会ですから選択の権限は男性にしかありませんでした。しかし，今はお互いを選ぶ権限はフィフティー・フィフティーです。むしろ，女性から三高のような条件を持ち出すようなお見合いであることが特徴ですが，さて，実際には恋愛結婚のほうが圧倒的ですから，現代女性はお見合いにはあまり期待をしていないのがホンネかもしれません。

Q Why do the Japanese have *omiai* even when they are still quite young?

A According to a survey carried out by the Ministry of Health and Welfare in 1987, love marriages comprised 74% of all couples getting married as opposed to arranged marriages which comprised 24%. However, according to a 1992 survey, the figures were 78% and 15%.

One of the prevalent preconceived notions that non-Japanese have about the Japanese is that all Japanese have *omiai* (an arranged meeting with a prospective marriage partner), but as the figures indicate, the number of people who actually have *omiai* has greatly decreased. But this is not to say that young Japanese women are negative about *omiai*.

For an unmarried young woman, the ideal marriage partner is one who is endowed with the "three highs" of high education, high salary and high stature (height). But finding such a person among prospective candidates close at hand is difficult. *Omiai* serves as a means of finding a suitable partner, and this concept has not changed even today.

The custom of *omiai* began among the common people during the Edo period (1600–1868), but in the male-dominated society, the right to choose was entirely the man's prerogative. Now, both men and women have an equal say in choosing a prospective partner, but it is usually the woman who brings up the three highs as a prerequisite. The large number of love marriages taking place may reflect the true feelings of the modern woman in not placing high expectations on an *omiai*.

英語で話す「日本の謎」Q&A
100 Tough Questions for Japan

1996年10月18日　第1刷発行
1998年10月20日　第11刷発行

監　修　板坂　元

編　集　株式会社　翻訳情報センター

発行者　野間佐和子

発行所　講談社インターナショナル株式会社
　　　　〒112-8652　東京都文京区音羽1-17-14
　　　　電話：03-3944-6493（編集）
　　　　　　　03-3944-6492（営業）

印刷所　大日本印刷株式会社

製本所　株式会社　堅省堂

落丁本、乱丁本は、講談社インターナショナル営業部宛にお送りください。送料小社負担にてお取替えいたします。なお、この本についてのお問い合わせは、編集局第二出版部宛にお願いいたします。本書の無断複写（コピー）は著作権法上での例外を除き、禁じられています。

定価はカバーに表示してあります。

Copyright ©1996 Kodansha International Ltd. and Translation Services, Inc.
ISBN4-7700-2091-0

講談社バイリンガル・ブックス

英語で読んでも面白い！

- 楽しく読めて自然に英語が身に付くバイリンガル表記
- 実用から娯楽まで読者の興味に応える多彩なテーマ
- 重要単語、表現法がひと目で分かる段落対応レイアウト

46判変型 (113 x 188 mm) 仮製

英語で話す「日本」Q&A
Talking About Japan Q & A

KBB 1

講談社インターナショナル 編　　　　　320ページ　ISBN 4-7700-2026-0

外国の人と話すとき、必ず出てくる話題は「日本」のこと。でも英語力よりも前に困るのは、日本について知らないことがいっぱいという事実です。政治、経済から文化までモヤモヤの知識をスッキリさせてくれる「日本再発見」の書。

英語で話す「アメリカ」Q&A
Talking About the USA Q & A

KBB 21

賀川 洋 著　　　　　312ページ　ISBN 4-7700-2005-8

仕事でも留学でも遊びでも、アメリカ人と交際するとき、知っておくと役に立つ「アメリカ小事典」。アメリカ人の精神と社会システムにポイントをおいた解説により、自然、歴史、政治、文化、そして人をバイリンガルで紹介します。

英語で話す「世界」Q&A
Talking About the World Q & A

KBB 19

講談社インターナショナル 編　　　　　320ページ　ISBN 4-7700-2006-6

今、世界にはいくつの国家があるか、ご存じですか？　対立をはらみながらも、急速に1つの運命共同体になっていく「世界」──外国の人と話すとき知らなければならない「世界」に関する国際人必携の「常識集」です。

英語で読む日本史
Japanese History : 11 Experts Reflect on the Past
KBB 4

英文日本大事典 編   232ページ   ISBN 4-7700-2024-4

11人の超一流ジャパノロジストたちが英語で書き下ろした日本全史。外国人の目から見た日本史はどういうものか、また日本の歴史事項を英語で何と表現するのか。新しい視点が想像力をかき立てます。

日本を創った100人
100 Japanese You Should Know
KBB 25

板坂 元 監修   英文日本大事典 編   240ページ   ISBN 4-7700-2159-3

混沌と激動を乗り越え築き上げられた現在の日本。その長い歴史の節目節目で大きな役割を果たした歴史上のキーパーソン100人を、超一流のジャパノロジストたちが解説。グローバルな大競争時代を迎えた今、彼らの生き方が大きな指針となります。

英語で話す「日本の謎」Q&A   外国人が聞きたがる100のWHY
100 Tough Questions for Japan
KBB 11

板坂 元 監修   248ページ   ISBN 4-7700-2091-0

なぜ、結婚式は教会で、葬式はお寺でなんてことができるの？   なぜ、大人までがマンガを読むの？   なぜ、時間とお金をかけてお茶を飲む練習をするの？──こんな外国人の問いをつきつめてゆくと、日本文化の核心が見えてきます。

英語で話す「日本の心」   和英辞典では引けないキーワード197
Keys to the Japanese Heart and Soul
KBB 12

英文日本大事典 編   328ページ   ISBN 4-7700-2082-1

一流のジャパノロジスト53人が解説した「日本の心」を知るためのキーワード集。「わび」「さび」「義理人情」「甘え」「根回し」「談合」「みそぎ」など、日本人特有な「心の動き」を外国人に説明するための強力なツールです。

英語で話す「日本の文化」
Japan as I See It
KBB 22

NHK国際放送局文化プロジェクト 編   ダン・ケニー 訳   208ページ   ISBN 4-7700-2197-6

金田一春彦、遠藤周作、梅原猛、平川祐弘、西堀栄三郎、鯖田豊之、野村万作、井上靖、小松左京、中根千枝の10人が、日本文化の「謎」を解く。NHKの国際放送で21の言語で放送され、分かりやすいと世界中で大好評。

ニッポン不思議発見！   日本文化を英語で語る50の名エッセイ集
Discover Japan: Words, Customs and Concepts
KBB 14

日本文化研究所 編   松本道弘 訳   272ページ   ISBN 4-7700-2142-9

絶望的な場合ですら、日本人は「そこをなんとか」という言葉を使って、相手に甘えようとする……こんな指摘をうけると、いかに日本人は独特なものの考え方をしているか分かります。あなたも「不思議」を発見してみませんか。

茶の本
The Book of Tea

KBB 28

岡倉天心 著　千 宗室 序と跋　浅野 晃 訳　　　264ページ　ISBN 4-7700-2379-0

一碗の茶をすする、そのささやかで簡潔な行為の中に、偉大な精神が宿っている——茶道によせて、日本と東洋の精神文化の素晴らしさを明かし、アジアの理想が回復されることを英文で呼びかけた本書は、日本の心を英語で明かす不朽の名著。

武士道
BUSHIDO

KBB 30

新渡戸稲造 著　須知徳平 訳　　　312ページ　ISBN 4-7700-2402-9

「日本が生んだ最大の国際人」新渡戸博士が英語で著した世界的名著。「日本の精神文化を知る最良の書」として世界17ヵ国語に翻訳され、1世紀にわたって読みつがれてきた不滅の日本人論。国際人必読の1冊。

「縮み」志向の日本人
Smaller is Better

KBB 33

李 御寧 著　　　200ページ　ISBN 4-7700-2445-2

一寸法師から、盆栽、箱庭、茶室、俳句にいたるまで、常に小さいものを求め、小さいものへ向かう「縮み志向」。言語・風俗・文化などが似ており、また日本文化にも影響を与えた韓国、その初代文化大臣を務めた著者によって発見された日本文化の本質。

ニッポン見聞録　大好きな日本人に贈る新・開国論
Heisei Highs and Lows

KBB 8

トム・リード 著　　　224ページ　ISBN 4-7700-2092-9

国際化の進む日本ですが、アメリカのジャーナリストが鋭い目と耳で浮き彫りにしたニッポンの姿は、驚くほど平穏でいとおしく、恥ずかしいくらい強欲で無知なものでした。トムが大好きな日本人へ贈る新・開国論。

「Japan」クリッピング　ワシントンポストが書いた「日本」
Views of Japan from The Washington Post Newsroom

KBB 6

東郷茂彦 著　　　264ページ　ISBN 4-7700-2023-6

アメリカの世論をリードするワシントン・ポストに書かれた「Japan」……政治、外交、経済、社会のジャンルで取り上げられた日本の姿を、国際ジャーナリストが解説し、その背後にある問題点を浮き彫りにする一冊。

開国ノススメ　孤立化するニッポンへの問題提起
Open Up, Japan!

KBB 31

アンドリュー・ホルバート 著　　　208ページ　ISBN 4-7700-2348-0

欧米の高級紙誌で活躍する一流の国際ジャーナリストが、海外で問われることの多い、日本の政治・経済・社会システムの問題について「どのように説明すればよいか」のヒントを与えてくれます。

NHK「ニュースのキーワード」
NHK: Key Words in the News
KBB 26

NHK国際放送局「ニュースのキーワード」プロジェクト 編　　232ページ　ISBN 4-7700-2342-1

日本で話題になっている時事問題を解説する、NHK国際放送の番組「ニュースのキーワード」から「総会屋」「日本版ビッグバン」「ダイオキシン」など、33のキーワードを収録しました。国際的観点からの解説が、現代の日本の姿を浮き彫りにします。

NHK「日本ひとくち歳時記」
Around the Year in Japan
KBB 32

NHK国際放送局「日本一口事典」プロジェクト 編　　256ページ　ISBN 4-7700-2457-6

ひな祭り、七夕、運動会、年賀状など季節感あふれる32のキーワードから、日本文化を斬新な視点で、簡潔に分かりやすく解説します。21ヵ国語で放送中のNHK国際放送局が発見した「ニッポン」。

ベスト・オブ・天声人語
VOX POPULI, VOX DEI
KBB 23

朝日新聞論説委員室 著　朝日イブニングニュース 訳　　288ページ　ISBN 4-7700-2166-6

「天声人語」は「朝日新聞」の名コラムというよりも、日本を代表するコラムです。香港返還、アムラー現象、たまごっち、マザー・テレサの死など、現代を読み解く傑作56編を、社会・世相、政治、スポーツなどのジャンル別に収録しました。

誤解される日本人　外国人がとまどう41の疑問
The Inscrutable Japanese
KBB 20

メリディアン・リソーシス・アソシエイツ 編　賀川 洋 著　　232ページ　ISBN 4-7700-2129-1

あなたのちょっとした仕草や表情が大きな誤解を招いているかもしれません。「日本人はどんなときに誤解を受けるのか?」そのメカニズムを解説し、「どのように外国人に説明すればよいか」最善の解決策を披露します。

ビジュアル 英語で読む日本国憲法
The Constitution of Japan
KBB 18

英文日本大百科事典 編　　208ページ　ISBN 4-7700-2191-7

難しいと思っていた「日本国憲法」も、英語で読むと不思議とよく分かります。日本国憲法を、59点の写真を使って、バイリンガルで分かりやすく解説しました。条文中に出てくる難解な日本語には、ルビや説明がついています。

イラスト 日本まるごと事典
Japan at a Glance
KBB 17

インターナショナル・インターンシップ・プログラムス 著　　256ページ（2色刷）　ISBN 4-7700-2080-5

1000点以上のイラストを使って日本のすべてを紹介——自然、文化、社会はもちろんのこと、折り紙の折り方、着物の着方から、ナベで米を炊く方法や「あっちむいてホイ」の遊び方まで国際交流に必要な知識とノウハウを満載。

英語で折り紙
Origami in English
KBB 3

山口 真 著　　　　　　　　　　168ページ　ISBN 4-7700-2027-9

たった一枚の紙から無数の造形が生まれ出る…･外国の人たちは、その面白さに目を見張ります。折るとき、英語で説明できるようにバイリンガルにしました。ホームステイ、留学、海外駐在に必携の一冊です。

英語で日本料理
100 Recipes from Japanese Cooking
KBB 15

辻調理師専門学校　畑耕一郎, 近藤一樹 著
　　　　　　　　272ページ（カラー口絵16ページ）　ISBN 4-7700-2079-1

外国の人と親しくなる最高の手段は、日本料理を作ってあげること、そしてその作り方を教えてあげることです。代表的な日本料理100品の作り方を、外国の計量法も入れながら、バイリンガルで分かりやすく説明します。

イラスト 日米ジェスチャー事典
The Illustrated Handbook of American and Japanese Gestures
KBB 34

スティーブン・N・ウイリアムス 著　　　264ページ　ISBN 4-7700-2344-8

知らなかったではすまされない——。誤解を受け、国際問題や大騒動を引き起こしかねない、日本とアメリカのジェスチャーの違いを、ひと目で分かるイラストで解説します。言葉よりモノをいう780のジェスチャー。

ドタンバのマナー
The Ultimate Guide to Etiquette in Japan
KBB 27

サトウサンペイ 著　　　240ページ（オールカラー）　ISBN 4-7700-2193-3

サンペイ流家元が自らしでかした「日常のヘマ」「海外でのヘマ」を一目で分かるようにマンガにした、フレッシュマンに贈る究極のマナー集。新社会人必読！知っていればすむことなのに、知らないために嫌われたり、憎まれてはかないません。

アメリカ日常生活のマナーＱ＆Ａ
Do As Americans Do
KBB 13

ジェームス・M・バーダマン, 倫子・バーダマン 著　　　264ページ　ISBN 4-7700-2128-3

"How do you do?" に "How do you do?" と答えてはいけないということ、ご存知でしたか？　日本では当たり前と思われていたことがマナー違反だったのです。旅行で、駐在で、留学でアメリカに行く人必携のマナー集。

日米比較 冠婚葬祭のマナー
Do It Right : Japanese & American Social Etiquette
KBB 2

ジェームス・M・バーダマン, 倫子・バーダマン 著　　　192ページ　ISBN 4-7700-2025-2

アメリカでは結婚式や葬式はどのように行われるのか？　お祝いや香典は？……そしてアメリカの人たちも、日本の事情を知りたがります。これだけあればもう困らない。日米冠婚葬祭マニュアル、バイリンガル版。

英語で話す「仏教」Q&A
Talking About Buddhism Q & A

KBB 24

高田佳人 著 ジェームス・M・バーダマン 訳　　　240ページ　ISBN 4-7700-2161-5

四十九日までに7回も法事をするのは、「亡くなった人が7回受ける裁判をこの世から
応援するため」だということ、ご存じでしたか？　これだけは知っておきたい「仏教」
に関することがらを、やさしい英語で説明できるようにした入門書です。

まんが 日本昔ばなし
Once Upon a Time in Japan

KBB 16

川内彩友美 編 ラルフ・マッカーシー 訳　　　160ページ　ISBN 4-7700-2173-9

人気テレビシリーズ「まんが日本昔ばなし」から、「桃太郎」「金太郎」「一寸法師」など、
より抜きの名作8話をラルフ・マッカーシーの名訳でお届けします。ホームステイな
どでも役に立つ一冊です。

まんが 日本昔ばなし 妖しのお話
Once Upon a Time in *Ghostly* Japan

KBB 29

川内彩友美 編 ラルフ・マッカーシー 訳　　　152ページ　ISBN 4-7700-2347-2

妖しく、怖く、心に響く昔ばなしの名作を英語で読む。人気テレビシリーズ「まんが
日本昔ばなし」から、「鶴の恩返し」「雪女」「舌切り雀」「耳なし芳一」「分福茶釜」など
8話を収録しました。

ベスト・オブ 宮沢賢治短編集
The Tales of Miyazawa Kenji

KBB 5

宮沢賢治 著 ジョン・ベスター 訳　　　216ページ　ISBN 4-7700-2081-3

「注文の多い料理店」「どんぐりと山猫」「祭の晩」「鹿踊りのはじまり」「土神ときつね」
「オツベルと象」「毒もみの好きな署長さん」「セロ弾きのゴーシュ」の代表作8編を精
選。ジョン・ベスターの名訳でどうぞ。

銀河鉄道の夜
Night Train to the Stars

KBB 10

宮沢賢治 著 ジョン・ベスター 訳　　　184ページ　ISBN 4-7700-2131-3

賢治童話の中でも最も人気の高い「銀河鉄道の夜」は、賢治の宗教心と科学精神が反
映された独特の世界——天空、自然、大地がみごとに描かれ、光と音と動きに満ち溢
れています。ジョバンニと一緒に銀河を旅してみませんか。

ベスト・オブ 窓ぎわのトットちゃん
Best of Totto-chan : The Little Girl at the Window

KBB 9

黒柳徹子 著 トロシー・ブリトン 訳　　　240ページ　ISBN 4-7700-2127-5

小学校一年生にして「退学」になったトットちゃんは、転校先の校長先生に「君は本
当はいい子なんだよ」と温かい言葉のシャワーで励まされます…バイリンガル版で、
あの空前の大ベストセラーの感動をもう一度！

マザー・グース　愛される唄70選
Mother Goose : 70 Nursery Rhymes

谷川俊太郎 訳　渡辺 茂 解説　　　　　　　　184ページ　ISBN 4-7700-2078-3

「マイ・フェア・レディー」や「お熱いのがお好き」という題名も、マザー・グースからの引用だったってこと、ご存じでしたか？ 英米人にとって必須教養であるこの童謡集を、詩人・谷川俊太郎の名訳と共にお楽しみください。

ビジネスマン必携！

対訳　英語で話す日本経済Q&A
A Bilingual Guide to the Japanese Economy

NHK国際放送局経済プロジェクト・
大和総研経済調査部 編
46判（128 x 188 mm）仮製　368ページ
ISBN 4-7700-1942-4

NHK国際放送で好評を得た番組が本になりました。クイズと会話形式で楽しく読んでいくうちに、日本経済の仕組が分かり、同時に英語にも強くなっていきます。日本語と英語の対応がひと目で分かる編集上の工夫もいっぱい。

名作＋名訳＋名画の魅力！

対訳　おくのほそ道
The Narrow Road to Oku

松尾芭蕉 著　ドナルド・キーン 訳
宮田雅之 切り絵
A5判変型（140 x 226 mm）
仮製　188ページ（カラー口絵41点）
ISBN 4-7700-2028-7

古典文学の最高峰のひとつ「おくのほそ道」をドナルド・キーンが新訳しました。画家、宮田雅之が精魂を込めた切り絵の魅力とあいまって、この名作に新しい生命が吹き込まれた、必読の1冊です。

対訳　竹取物語
The Tale of the Bamboo Cutter

川端康成 現代語訳　ドナルド・キーン 英訳
宮田雅之 切り絵
A5判変型・横長（226 x 148 mm）
仮製　箱入り 180ページ（カラー口絵16点）
ISBN 4-7700-2329-4

ノーベル賞作家の現代語訳と傑出した芸術家の作品、そして日本文学の研究に一生を捧げたジャパノロジストの翻訳が合体した、大人のための「竹取物語」。

講談社バイリンガル・コミックス

英語と日本語で楽しむ

対訳 サザエさん (全12巻)
The Wonderful World of Sazae-san

長谷川町子 著　ジュールス・ヤング 訳

- 吹き出しの中にオリジナルの暖かい雰囲気を大切にした英語、コマの横に日本語がつく対訳形式。

- お正月、こいのぼり、忘年会など日本独特の文化や習慣には、欄外に英語の解説つき。

46判変型（113 x 188 mm）仮製

完全対訳のバイリンガル事典、誕生。

対訳 日本事典 (全1巻)
The Kodansha Bilingual Encyclopedia of Japan

講談社インターナショナル 編

B5判（182 x 257 mm）
上製 箱入り
944ページ（カラー口絵16ページ）
ISBN 4-7700-2130-5

ビジネス、海外駐在、
留学、ホームステイなど、
さまざまな国際交流の場で、
幅広くご活用いただけます。

特色

「日本」を国際的な視点で理解できる幅広い知識と、
実用的な英語が身につきます。

1. 現代の政治制度、最新の経済情報を豊富に記載し、日本を総
   合的に理解できる。
2. 分野別の構成により、テーマに沿って自然に読み進むことが
   できる。
3. 豊富なイラストと図版を収録し、完全対訳のレイアウトと欄
   外のキーワードで、重要単語や表現の日英相互参照に便利。
4. 日本国憲法、重要な国際条約、年表をいずれも日英併記で巻
   末に収録。
5. 英語からも日本語（ローマ字）からも引けるインデックスつき。

内容構成

地理 / 歴史 / 政治 / 経済 / 社会 / 文化 / 生活

楽しく読んで英語が身につく
講談社英語文庫
Kodansha English Library

 特色

古典から最新話題作まで、幅広いジャンルの作品が英語で読めます。

英語の初心者から上級者まで十分読みごたえのある、さまざまなレベルの作品が揃っています。

なるべく辞書を使わずに楽しく読めるよう、原則として巻末にNotes(語句の解説)をつけてあります。

人気イラストレーターによる美しい装画、さし絵が人気です。

比較的大きめの活字を使った、読みやすい英文が好評です。

☆印は英語のレベルを表わしています。☆の数が多くなるほどレベルが上がります。

海外の作品

パトリシア・コーンウェル	検屍官 I	☆☆☆☆
	検屍官 II	☆☆☆☆
J・D・サリンジャー	ライ麦畑でつかまえて	☆☆☆☆
	ナイン・ストーリーズ	☆☆☆☆
ウイリアム・サローヤン	パパ・ユーア クレイジー	☆☆
エリック・シーガル	ラブ・ストーリィ	☆☆☆
アーウィン・ショー	夏服を着た女たち	☆☆☆☆
ズフェルト	星占いの本	☆☆
チャールズ・ディケンズ	クリスマス・キャロル	☆☆
コナン・ドイル	シャーロック・ホームズの冒険	☆☆☆
マーク・トウェーン	トム・ソーヤーの冒険	☆☆
P・L・トラヴァース	メアリー・ポピンズ	☆☆
C・W・ニコル	風を見た少年	☆☆
L・フランク・バーム	オズの魔法使い	☆☆
ラフカディオ・ハーン	怪談	☆☆☆
ピート・ハミル	ニューヨーク・スケッチブック	☆☆☆☆
J・M・バリ	ピーター・パン	☆☆
F・スコット・フィッツジェラルド	華麗なるギャツビー	☆☆☆☆
アラン・ブース	マクベス*	☆☆
アーネスト・ヘミングウェイ	老人と海	☆☆☆
O・ヘンリー	O・ヘンリー短編集	☆☆☆
カースティン・マカイヴァー	聖書ものがたり*	☆☆
	聖書の名言集*	☆☆
ラルフ・マッカーシー	イソップ物語*	☆
	アラビアンナイト*	☆☆
	ギリシャ神話*	☆☆
	アメリカ昔ばなし*	☆☆
A・A・ミルン	クマのプーさん	☆☆
	プー横丁にたった家	☆☆
サマセット・モーム	モーム短編集	☆☆☆
L・M・モンゴメリ	赤毛のアン	☆☆☆
	続・赤毛のアン	☆☆☆
トーベ・ヤンソン	たのしいムーミン一家	☆☆
キャサリン・ルビンスタイン	ラブレターズ	☆☆☆☆
ローラ・インガルス・ワイルダー	大草原の小さな家	☆☆
オスカー・ワイルド	幸福な王子	☆☆☆
(絵) 小林与志	マザーグース	☆
	マザーグース 2	☆
	マザーグース 3	☆

*印は、原作をもとに英語文庫のために書き下ろした作品です